PREHISTORIC LOCATIONAL BEHAVIOR:
A COMPUTER SIMULATION

PREHISTORIC LOCATIONAL BEHAVIOR: A COMPUTER SIMULATION

LARRY J. ZIMMERMAN

Report 10
Office of the State Archaeologist
The University of Iowa
Iowa City
1977

Prehistoric Locational Behavior: A Computer Simulation
Larry J. Zimmerman
*Tenth in a series of reports issued at intervals
by the Office of the State Archaeologist
The University of Iowa
Iowa City*

DUANE C. ANDERSON, *State Archaeologist*
ELKA GRISHAM, *Editor*

Library of Congress Cataloging in Publication Data

Zimmerman, Larry J.   1947-
    Prehistoric locational behavior.

    (Report—Office of the State Archaeologist ; 10)
    Bibliography: p.
    1. Indians of North America—Iowa—Mills Co.
2. Anthropo-geography—Data processing. 3. Archaeology—Data processing. 4. Iowa—Antiquities.
5. Mills Co., Iowa—Antiquities. I. Title.
II. Series: Iowa. State Archaeologist. Report ; 10.
E78.I6Z55   977.7'74   77-8440
ISBN 0-87414-004-8

In Memory of
AUGUST DIETRICH ZIMMERMAN

Table of Contents

List of Figures   viii
List of Tables   ix
Acknowledgements   x
Introduction   xi
1   Concepts and Approaches in the Study of
     Locational Behavior   1
2   The Modelling Process   16
3   Simulation of Human Behavioral Phenomena   26
4   Changing Concepts of Settlement Patterns
     in the Glenwood Locality   34
5   Modelling Goals   41
6   Systems Analysis   45
7   System Synthesis   83
8   Verification   96
9   Validation and Initial Inferences   101
10   Inferences about Locational Behavior in the
     Glenwood Locality   122
11   The Efficacy of Simulating Locational Processes   128
Appendix: Glenwood I Program List   137
Bibliography   159

List of Figures

Figure

1	The Modelling Process	20
2	Simplified Flow Chart for Simulation of Settlement Subsistence Systems	43
3	Anderson's 1961 Map of the Glenwood Locality	46
4	Computer Generated Contour Map of the Glenwood Locality	60
5	Three-Dimensional Projection of the Glenwood Locality: Elevation 60.0	61
6	Three-Dimensional projection of the Glenwood Locality: Elevation 45.0	62
7	The Woman Node Concept	88
8	Territory Claimed by Lodges A.D. 910	93
9	Known Distribution of Earthlodges in the Glenwood Locality	104
10	Simulated Distribution of Earthlodges: Run A	107
11	Population Curve: Run A	108
12	Simulated Distribution of Earthlodges: Run B	110
13	Simulated Distribution of Earthlodges: Run C	112
14	Simulated Distribution of Earthlodges: Run D	114
15	Simulated Distribution of Earthlodges: Run E	115
16	Simulated Distribution of Earthlodges: Run F	117
17	Simulated Distribution of Earthlodges: Run G	118
18	Population Curve: Run G	120
19	Simulated Distribution of Earthlodges: Run G1	121

List of Tables

Table
1   Exemplary Models   18
2   Mammalian Fauna from Glenwood Locality
    Earthlodges by Community Association   55
3   Table of First Parturition (TPART)   67
4   Female (WMARG) and Male (MMARG)
    Table of Marriage   68
5   Female (WMORT) and Male (MMORT)
    Table of Mortality   69
6   Radiocarbon Dates from the Glenwood Locality   126

ACKNOWLEDGEMENTS: The Glenwood locality has been, and to some extent remains, an enigma as one of the easternmost extensions of Central Plains tradition culture. Its precise origins are not clear nor is its disappearance. Caddoan influence is clear as is contact with groups of Great Oasis and Oneota cultural affiliation. These historical questions are not, however, addressed in this book. The problem considered here is perhaps less exotic, but is as important. The primary concern is to explain the integration of cultural components with locational behavior manifest in settlement patterns. Analysis of these matters uses a relatively new approach in archaeology: computer simulation. For me, the approach was very stimulating; the results, I hope, will be useful and will provide a focal point for further research in the Glenwood locality.

The research reported here is the result of assistance from many individuals. My advisor and dissertation supervisor, Dr. Alfred Johnson, must be credited for his willingness to allow my pursuit of unorthodox ideas and for his perceptive criticisms. Drs. Anta White and Robert Nunley did a masterful job of pushing an at-first unwilling student into realms of geography that ultimately provided countless ideas and inspirations. Drs. Carlyle Smith and Robert Squier provided thought-provoking seminars that helped me better view my work in historical perspective.

Elka Grisham, Office of the State Archaeologist of Iowa, was a perceptive and helpful editor. Several individuals read the manuscript and provided useful comment and encouragement. They were: Duane Anderson, State Archaeologist of Iowa; Robert Alex, State Historical Department of Iowa, Division of Historic Preservation; and R. Clark Mallam, Luther College. Waldo and Mildred Mott Wedel provided a word of encouragement that meant more to me than they probably realized. J. E. Doran, Computing Centre, University of Essex, offered excellent comments and criticisms. Lawrence Bradley, Darrell Fulmer, and Paul Brockington often acted as valuable sounding boards for ideas. John Hotopp provided radiocarbon dates from his recent excavations in the Glenwood locality. Karen Pike Zimmerman typed the manuscript in its various stages. Her encouragement and light-hearted comments about writing archaeological science fiction were extremely important to me.

Support for my research came from many sources. They include the Society of the Sigma Xi; The University of Kansas, both for a summer fellowship and computer time via the Departments of Anthropology and Computer Science; the Office of the State Archaeologist of Iowa; the Midwest Archaeological Center of the National Park Service; and the Iowa State Highway Commission. Finally, through support as a research associate of the Institute of Indian Studies, The University of South Dakota, I was allowed to complete my research.

Collaboration with two individuals merits special mention here. Dr. Daniel Moore, Department of Computer and Information Sciences, Ohio State University, steered me toward the use of SIMSCRIPT. Dan worked diligently on the programming of the prototype for Glenwood I and the debugging of Glenwood I itself. He taught me a great deal about programming and I thank him for his patience and his interest in my research. Dr. Adrian Anderson, State Historical Department of Iowa, Division of Historic Preservation, acted as a good teacher and friend. He willingly provided information from his own research into the Glenwood locality. Several of his ideas, hopefully represented correctly, are incorporated here. The positive contribution of these two individuals cannot be overstated; without their efforts this work would no doubt have been vastly different or not written at all.

The Glenwood "bluffs" are considerably changed from what they were prehistorically; yet, they remain to me mysterious and majestic. They impart a certain *mana* to me each time I drive near them. I hope I have done them justice herein and conveyed some of their splendor to the reader.

Introduction

By 1911, Gilder (1911:249) was referring to earthlodge remains in eastern Nebraska as a "culture." He was not explicit in his application of the term, but did describe and illustrate artifacts and structures from the region along the west bank of the Missouri River in Nebraska. He pointed out that these archaeological materials were different from those across the Missouri River in Iowa (1911:252; 1913:116). Sterns's excavations of the "Gilderite Culture" in Nebraska further defined the archaeological characteristics of the "culture," but as well as noting similarities to materials across the river in Iowa, he also noted local variations (Gradwohl 1969:37). These manifestations are nominally components of the Nebraska phase of the Central Plains tradition.

Although the contemporary taxonomic terminology applied to Gilder's "culture" is somewhat controversial (Gradwohl 1969:35-62; Krause 1969:82-96), the characteristics that define the "culture" are moderately well established. Those discussed by Wedel (1959:560-562, 566) and others (Strong 1935; Gradwohl 1969) include:

1) A subsistence economy divided about equally between maize horticulture and hunting.
2) Grit-tempered pottery with cord-roughened or smoothed surfaces. Rims on these vessels are usually simple vertical to flared with no decoration or collared with cord-impressed or incised decoration. Some shell-tempered vessels occur.
3) Small triangular chipped projectile points with no side or side-and-base notching.
4) Scapula hoes.
5) Square to rectangular semisubterranean earthlodges with rounded corners, four central roof supports around a central fireplace, and an extended entryway.
6) Sites occurring commonly on narrow ridges, although sometimes occurring on hillslopes and terraces of major streams tributary to the Missouri River.
7) Sites usually found as straggling lines of house pits, rarely in groups, and seldom as compact settlements. Isolated houses also occur.

xi

The first six characteristics are generally accepted as accurately descriptive; the seventh has recently been challenged.

Gradwohl (1969:2, 135) indirectly challenged the existence of a dispersed form of settlement distribution. He felt that the normal pattern was simply a small cluster of houses and viewed the dispersed, isolated pattern as an artifact of survey techniques, selective excavation, and the practice of numbering each house in a site as a single site. Through time, and affected further by taxonomic strictures, the dispersed pattern became more an undemonstrated mental construct than a spatial reality. In light of Gradwohl's statements and seemingly contradictory evidence from other Central Plains tradition localities (Wood 1969; Krause 1970), Anderson and Zimmerman (n.d.) chose to reexamine the distribution of earthlodges in the Glenwood locality of Mills County in southwest Iowa.

Anderson and Zimmerman noted that two forms of settlement appeared in the Glenwood locality: the dispersed variety, isolated lodges strung along ridgelines; and the nucleated form, small clusters of lodges located on hillslopes or stream terraces. They therefore concluded that the earlier emphasis on the dispersed pattern was overstated and that Gradwohl was correct in pointing out the frequency of the clustered form. They further offered a loosely structured, speculative model to account for the development of both forms. Their model was generally descriptive, but did attempt to delimit variables and their interrelationships; the model was, as they structured it, difficult to test. If such variability in the settlement pattern exists, the processes by which it came to be must be delineated and tested. The explanation of settlement variability in the Glenwood locality will be the focal problem of this work.

To explain Glenwood settlement variability, three issues must ultimately be considered. The first is the need for a general understanding of prehistoric locational behavior and spatial processes. The second is the necessity for generating a theoretical framework and methodology that will aid in visualizing the processes at work, handle a large number of variables, and have explanatory capabilities. Finally, within the framework of these two issues, the particular circumstances of the Glenwood locality must be dealt with.

Chapters 1 and 2 address the first and second issues above. Chapter 1, Concepts and Approaches in the Study of Prehistoric Locational Behavior, discusses relevant archaeological concepts from settlement archaeology concerned with locational behavior. This chapter also considers the role of geographic concepts and models of locational behavior and spatial process in the development of such concepts for archaeology. Chapter 2, The Modelling Process, and Chapter 3, Simulation of Human Behavioral Phenomena, are largely methodological. The utility of model building, following Mihram (1972a), is discussed in detail, and a particular model form, the simular model, is examined for its potential application to locational problems. The intent of both chapters is to suggest that computer simulation would be beneficial in solving the problems of explaining Glenwood settlement variability specifically and prehistoric locational behavior in general.

Chapters 4 through 10 are concerned with the application of simular modelling to the Glenwood settlement problem. Chapter 4 deals with the archaeological background of the problem and is largely historiographic in nature. The development of concepts about Central Plains tradition settlement patterns and, specifically, the developments leading to the Anderson-Zimmerman model for the Glenwood locality are discussed. Chapters 5 through 10 are organized around Mihram's stages of the modelling process. Chapter 5 considers modelling goals. Chapter 6, an analysis of the Glenwood settlement system, is subdivided into discussions of the system's various components and their interrelationships. Chapter 7 is concerned with synthesis of the model through the use of the computer language SIMSCRIPT. Chapter 8 is an attempt to verify the synthesized model and a discussion of programming intricacies and difficulties. Chapter 9 deals with validation of the model. Chapter 10 details inferences about Glenwood locational behavior and discusses experimentation with the model based on those inferences.

Chapter 11 is an assessment of the efficacy of simulation modelling for the particular problem and for archaeological investigations of prehistoric locational behavior in general. Suggestions for further research are also offered. Conclusions and a summary recap the major points of this work.

The Anderson-Zimmerman model will provide the core for the explanation of Glenwood settlement variability; it will be modified, phrased in deductive terms, and most importantly, operationalized using simulation techniques. The implications of that simulation will be analyzed and an estimation of the model's validity offered. Although the anthropological problem of settlement variability is the key issue under consideration, the methodological structures used will merit scrutiny. Discussions of settlement processes in the Glenwood locality will therefore be illuminated against the background of a synthetic approach to settlement patterns and the relatively new archaeological realm of simular modelling. A better understanding of prehistoric locational behavior and approaches to analysis of it is the ultimate goal.

1.   Concepts and Approaches in the Study of Locational Behavior

The perplexing question of why people locate themselves where they do has been a relatively recent focus for prehistory, in vogue only since the development of settlement pattern analysis as an important area of research in the early 1950's (Willey 1953, 1956). With the recent concern for delineation and explanation of cultural processes, research on prehistoric locational analysis has become the focal point for entire regional research efforts (Gumerman 1971). That the question is important is obvious: an individual or aggregate has to be somewhere exploiting the environment and relating to cultural contemporaries in specified ways. In many respects, therefore, human location can be seen as an integrative mechanism, a point of articulation for several cultural subsystems; position on the landscape is the locus, the spatial dimension, of all human activity. Analysis of one aspect of this spatial dimension, the locational decision, is of particular importance here.

The imperatives involved in a locational decision are relatively few; those that operate do so within a framework of environmentally and culturally delimited parameters that are functionally set by systemic mutual interaction. To know what these imperatives are, let alone the particulars of the parameters, is difficult and perhaps impossible, even when one is personally involved in making the decision.

People have, in other words, an idea of location in terms of where persons in their "situation" should or would like to live. In general they know the major factors that contribute to their idea of location—income, availability of key resources, distance to relatives and friends, for example—those elements that combine in such a way as to provide locations that are acceptable according to standards of a culturally defined "quality of life." Within a set of locations that minimally meet these standards, those major factors, the imperatives, can be seen as flexible to be manipulated or juggled until an acceptable combination is found. In Western cultures it is often acceptable to pay a little more rent, as long as it does not exceed a certain limit necessary to maintain other standards of

1

living, in order to be a little closer to one's place of employment. One might also pay a little more for a larger residence, one with furniture or a nice view. On the other hand, one might pay little money for a less than luxurious farm outside the city to be away from crowds and noises as long as it is not too far from one's place of work. These imperatives have ultimate boundaries; as one of these boundaries is approached in a locational decision, the other imperatives fluctuate in proportion. These parameters, as noted above, are functionally set by interaction with each other. The parameters are "fuzzy" and complicated by mutual interaction, by factors of lesser importance (e.g., how many windows, what kind of furnace), and by a number of seemingly random factors (e.g., those variables that determine what places are advertised for rent on a particular day).

Within this framework people make locational decisions. They control only a few of the variables and know only in a general way the parameters of the imperatives and the standards of acceptable living. The random factors they can seldom control and rarely consider. Yet they do make functional choices. Analyzing these decisions is difficult even for the decision makers themselves. Questions raised about locational behavior have been considered by many disciplines. Some of those important to the study of prehistoric locational behavior are discussed in this chapter.

Locational Theory and Archaeology: Settlement Archaeology as Geography

That geographic considerations have become important is indicated by their inclusion in basic archaeological text materials. Hole and Heizer (1973:354-362) include as part of their text a major departure from their earlier edition (1965). This departure focuses attention on settlement patterns with a new orientation on spatial analysis from geography and its potential application to archaeology. Hole and Heizer suggest that archaeological concerns with human location, couched in the framework of traditional settlement pattern studies, dealt primarily with man-land relationships believed to operate as part of an adaptive system. Geographers are attributed a greater concern with man-man relationships operating in an economic or information network. Archaeology was focused on real data and explanation of particular instances, while geography was concerned with statistical data and attempted to understand classes of events through the use of abstract models (Hole and Heizer 1973:360-361). Perhaps these characteristics are a bit monolithic, but Hole and Heizer do offer that the two fields are not intrinsically incompatible and suggest that there is evidence that the approaches are converging.

The statements of two other individuals, one an archaeologist and the other a geographer, complement Hole and Heizer's statements. Judge (1971:38) notes that ". . . ultimately we must attempt to explain the process of culture change involved in the transition from one type of settlement to another." Morrill (1965:14) makes a similar statement that mirrors the characterization of Hole and Heizer. He says, "The search for simple theoretical notions of how settlement patterns in general develop is therefore the dominant goal [of this work]. The test of actual success is whether the actual pattern could have been produced by the suggested theory." The concerns of the two are the same: explanation of settlement pattern development. The former statement is that of an archaeologist and is relatively nonspecific in terminology; the latter is that of the geographer and is both a proposal of problem and methodology as well as a concern for a specific set of data.

Hole and Heizer (1973:360) are not incorrect in their assessment of the differences in concept of archaeological and geographical concerns with space and its use. The problems of dealing with Western industrialized cultures are different from those related to hunter/gatherers and horticulturalists. Most geographic models, concepts, and methods concerned with utilization of space are applicable to archaeological problems with very little change except scale. The two disciplines do share a common heritage and have influenced each other at several times in their development. In fact, the development of settlement archaeology has been directly subject to the influence of geography. Brief analysis of the rise of settlement studies in archaeology might be of use to demonstrate the shared conceptual bases of settlement studies in both disciplines.

Development of Conceptual Foundations in Settlement Archaeology

The development of studies in settlement archaeology can be seen as a peculiarly American phenomenon. Systematic applications of the settlement approach have been rare in Old World studies until recent years. The approach is not, however, without some Old World antecedents. Indeed, settlement archaeological concepts appeared in the development of cultural geography in Europe in the late 19th century, continued through the work of a few early and mid-20th century Old World archaeologists, and emerged after 1950 in conjunction with the locational analytical and theoretical development of modern European geography. The purpose of this perspective is to outline the development of settlement archaeology with particular emphasis on its links with geography and the

4

academic climate in which the approach was conceptualized and expanded. Since the major early developments were from New World anthropological archaeology, they will be emphasized.

The concepts of "settlement archaeology" and "settlement pattern" were first systematically applied to archaeological data by Gordon Willey (1953), but the idea of "settlement" was not particularly new at that time. Since the 19th century, the term "settlement" had been used in descriptions of cultures to distinguish sites with habitation debris (settlement sites) from non-occupation sites. To some extent "settlement" still maintains that meaning in both the Old and New Worlds (see for example Piggot 1965:40). "Distribution of settlements" in the Old World generally refers to the geographical distribution of artifacts and other tangible remains in locations where there is evidence that domestic activities were carried out (Tringham 1972:xix). Old World concerns with settlement have had a more spatial or locatory basis than those of New World archaeology.

Willey (1953:1) defines settlement patterns ". . . as the way in which man disposed himself over the landscape on which he lived." At that point his concern was locatory, but he continues:

> It refers to dwellings, to their arrangement, and to the nature and disposition of other buildings pertaining to community life. These settlements reflect the natural environment, the level of technology on which the builders operated, and various institutions of social interaction and control which the culture maintained. Because settlement patterns are, to a large extent, directly shaped by widely held cultural needs, they offer a strategic starting point for the functional interpretation of archaeological cultures.

His concern becomes more than spatial-analytical and is extended to include the study of environmental, technological, and social factors. He suggests that human settlement is a function of man/environment interaction and is therefore a point of articulation for all those factors, making them easily accessible to the archaeologist. As Willey (1953:19-23) demonstrates, settlement patterns provide one of the strongest links between archaeology and ethnography. His concept of settlement is that shared by most New World archaeologists and recently by many Old World specialists.

The idea that settlement is a point of articulation for society and environment first appeared in the late 19th century when florescent ethnographic and geographic studies of non-Western cultures were linked with the rise of ideas of unilinear evolution. While ethnography was more concerned with description of cultural variety, geography was generally more concerned with the reasons for the variety and with the influences of environment on human culture.

The first major systematic study of human geography was conducted by the German, Friedrich Ratzel, who coined the word "anthropogeography" as a label for his work. Ratzel (1899) formulated concepts concerning land settlement that were focused particularly on the culture of man rather than the physical features of the earth and especially on man in relation to the environment. He also dealt with the geographic patterns resulting from contact between groups of humans, especially between aggressive, expanding cultures and those that were weaker and submissive (Ratzel 1896:79). Although Harris (1968:383) describes Ratzel's concerns as "eclectic," his concerns with human migration and diffusionary processes place Ratzel in the forefront of those dealing with human geographic distributions and explanation of those distributions in both environmental and cultural terms. Parenthetically, many of Ratzel's ideas concerning man-land interaction appear to be the result of his travels and studies in the United States, especially his work on the Indians of the Southwest (Sauer 1971). Brief summaries and critiques of Ratzel's work are to be found in Lowie (1937), Hartshorne (1958), and James (1972). Ratzel's work was embellished in Europe by Hettner (1907), who continued to focus on man's relation to his physical environment and particularly on possible causal factors (James 1972:228).

American geographers and anthropologists were exposed to anthropogeography mainly through the work of one of Ratzel's students, Ellen Semple (1911). Others to whom Americans were exposed early were Vidal de la Blache (1926), who was directly concerned with shelter and human habitats, and the Russian, Voeikov (James 1972), who was concerned with the influences of man on the environment. Although no direct connections have been demonstrated between the early European anthropogeographers (except slightly later through Semple) and the American ethnographers, overlapping concerns can be seen in Morgan's (1881) aboriginal house studies and Mindeleff's (1900) work on the distribution of Pueblo ruins in the Southwest. To Morgan and Mindeleff, Chang (1972:1) attributes the first American interests in habitation and architecture.

The work of the anthropogeographers, especially Ratzel, fueled the flames of the ideas of diffusion, especially the hyperdiffusionism of Smith (1930) and Perry (1924); but in part, those ideas were probably also the basis for modified diffusion schemes such as those of Childe (1925, 1958). The intent here is not to overemphasize the diffusion aspects of anthropogeography, but simply to point out the early concern with explanation of spatial distribution of cultural traits.

The ideas of man-land interaction as explanatory mechanisms remain the key source for settlement studies and were perhaps the main contribution of the anthropogeographers. In Europe, those concepts were most important for the development of economic analyses of archaeological data as applied by Childe (1935, 1946) and Clark (1952, 1968). Childe's viewpoint is essentially materialistic; he suggests that culture is largely a response to environment (1946:15) and that material culture ultimately influences all other aspects of culture. Clark's analytical approach is that of economic reconstruction as the basis of archaeological interpretation, and from that base stem reconstructions of other aspects of culture (ideology, art, etc.). Clark views shelter and ecological factors as part of economy. Although Childe and Clark are similar in their orientation toward the economic aspects of culture, Clark in particular seems to share the concepts of settlement archaeology held by most American archaeologists (see Clark 1968:169-224, esp. 175-199 and 219-220) even though he does not use the terminology. Both Childe and Clark use the term "settlement" to mean habitation sites with some type of fabricated shelters (Childe 1956:49; Clark 1968:198). With few other exceptions, the settlement approach in Old World studies is so rare, even when couched in terms of economic analysis, that it is seldom mentioned in historical views of Old World archaeology (e.g., Daniel 1967, 1968). Finally, it should be noted that these concerns with settlement in economic terms were being developed during roughly the same time period as the development of settlement archaeology in the Americas.

Even though there appear to be antecedents of an archaeological nature for the development of settlement archaeology in both the Old and New World, the settlement pattern as a focused methodological research concept was not brought to the forefront until Willey (1953) applied it in the Viru Valley project of the Institute of Andean Research. Willey's (1974) own retrospective concerning his role in the project is enlightening.

In the fall of 1945, the idea of concentrated archaeological and ethnographic study of a single Peruvian coastal valley was put forward by W. C. Bennett in conversations with Willey and Julian Steward. Willey's personal inclination was to work with Ford on stratigraphic analyses of test pits at selected sites. Willey (1974:153) says:

It was at this point that Julian Steward stepped in and convinced me that it would be the better part of archaeological wisdom if I withdrew from the "stratigraphic race" and conducted what he referred to as a settlement pattern survey. . . . I would be doing more for the project, myself, and archeology, he argued, if I attempted to say something about the forms, settings, and spatial relationships of sites themselves and what all this might imply about the societies which constructed and lived in them.

Willey claimed not to realize the research and integrative potential of his study.

I felt I had been misled by Steward and dealt a marginal hand by my colleagues. . . . I was chasing some kind of a wraith called "settlement patterns" that had been dreamed up by a social anthropologist (Willey 1974:154).

Willey's (1953) Viru Valley report tends to demonstrate just that. The report is very much descriptive and tends to assign only functional labels to the kinds of settlement he found (fortification, pyramids, etc.). Willey suggests that his interpretations could have been infinitely greater; indeed, they represent only a small segment of the finished report (1953:342-395).

Willey's analysis of the intellectual climate of the late 1940's sheds further light on the development of the settlement approach. He cites the work of Kluckholn and Steward in the 1930's and early 1940's as influential, especially their emphasis on functional interpretation and processes, which reached fruition in Taylor's (1948) publication. There seemed to be a general feeling that archaeology should be more than descriptive and chronological studies. Willey emphasizes the influence of Steward's (1938) monograph on Great Basin ethnology and his "Ecological Aspects of Southwestern Society" (1937). In these works, Steward discusses the constraints of natural environment and subsistence adaptations on the development of socioeconomic forms. The environmental and socio-cultural relationships were revealed in settlement distributions over the wider landscape as well as in the single community. In essence, then, and by Willey's own admission, the advent of settlement archaeology was from the early developments in cultural ecology, precisely the sort of approach discussed by the anthropogeographers. It is also interesting to note that on the Viru Valley project, Steward's field representative was F. W. McBryde, a cultural geographer.

By the mid-1950's, Steward's work had gained general acceptance in anthropology, as had Willey's settlement pattern studies, but with limited acclaim. The implications of ecological studies in archaeology, especially in terms of community patterning, were discussed in the 1955 Society for American Archeology Symposium (Beardsley 1956) concerned with the functional and evolutionary implications of community patterning. The major concern was a classification of cultures usable for both ethnographic and archaeological materials. They defined seven primary types of community patterns (free wandering, restricted wandering, central based wandering, semi-permanent sedentary, simple nuclear centered, advanced nuclear centered, and super-nuclear integrated) and suggested the correlation of these types to particular subsistence strategies, viewing subsistence base as a functional explanation for the variability (Beardsley 1956:150). For each of the categories, several ethnographic and archaeological examples were given. Also published in 1956 was the Willey edited volume, *Prehistoric Settlement Patterns in the New World*, which contained a series of descriptive papers covering most of the New World culture areas. Only Wedel's paper on the Plains and the one by Meggers and Evans on tropical forest zones had particularly ecological bases. Little effort had been expended in either the SAA Symposium or the Willey volume to draw any conclusions concerning social aspects of culture from archaeological data, although the possibility was thought to exist.

In 1958, Chang published his "Study of New World Social Groupings: Examples from the New World" and brought the settlement pattern into view as a means of reconstructing social organization from archaeological data. In his paper he used ethnographic data, and archaeologists were still wanting for an archaeological example. In *Rethinking Archaeology*, Chang (1967) outlined in detail his conceptual framework. He viewed the sociological concept of community as the proper basis for a unit through which archaeologists could examine the social context in which artifacts were created, a unit that was easily discoverable. Chang (1968:2) saw the community as a universal: "it defines the boundaries of social activities an individual daily engages in, and it molds or conditions an individual's mode of behavior and his view of life and the world perhaps more effectively than any other primary or secondary social group." Archaeologically, the community is the most definable social group, the locus of which is the settlement. Chang (1968:3) defines settlement as "the physical locale or cluster of locales where the members of a community lived, ensured their subsistence and pursued their social functions in a delineable time period." Chang's definition is more inclusive than Willey's in that even though settlement arrangements were said to be related to the adjustments of man and culture to environment, settlement patterns were still classified in much the same way as artifacts. Emphasis was usually focused on one time period. Chang, even though he viewed settlement as a system, failed to delineate the components of that system in a precise way so that his definitions could be operationalized. Chang also treated settlement as another form of artifact to be described and classified in order to determine genetic or generic relationships between groups or to establish culture histories. In all fairness, it should be noted that Chang is largely responsible for creating interest in analysis of settlement patterns for the reconstruction of social organization.

Only in the most general sense have archaeologists been primarily concerned with the causal factors that determine settlement or initiate settlement change. Trigger (1968) came the closest to delineating settlement determinants in any precise way. He says that settlement determinants ". . . are those classes of factors that interact with each other to produce the spatial configurations of a social group" (Trigger 1968:53). He analyzed settlement on three levels: the individual structure or building, the manner in which the structures are arranged within single communities, and the manner in which the communities are distributed over the landscape. For each of the levels he listed a number of determinants (e.g., climate, technological level, social organization, residence patterns), but failed to provide a mechanism for analysis of the determinants and their interactions. What Trigger approached, but still lacked, was an attachment of concepts to a definite theoretical construct. He partially operationalized the concept of settlement, but his determinants remain simply a list of factors that contribute to the locational decisions made by individuals in communities.

The conceptualization of settlement as the result of a number of intimately interacting components fits nicely into the structure of culture as a dynamic system. Culture as a system is not new to anthropology, but few outright attempts at systems analyses have been made. Most anthropologists seem to understand the basic concepts of systems theory, but have been reticent to attempt analyses, perhaps because cultural systems have been viewed as intractable due to the immense number of variables involved. To date, most settlement studies have been descriptive in nature and several have attempted to understand the linkages between the factors that determine settlement. Many articles have been published that analyze a whole range of settlement related phenomena (e.g., Chang 1968). These have been attempts by archaeologists to work out the determinants of settlement on their own. Only recently have archaeologists realized that modern geography covered much of the same ground ten years ago.

Attempts by archaeologists to understand the processes of the human locational decision have been few. In fact, little has been done to reach an adequate understanding of human spatial distribution. Although not directly concerned with prehistoric populations, the discipline of geography has at least used spatial distribution as its unifying theme (Berry 1968:25). Only since 1970 have archaeologists begun to use the vast store of geographic resources, especially techniques and models that are directly concerned with human settlement.

The major work in geography that is cited by many archaeologists is Haggett's (1965) *Locational Analysis in Human Geography*, which is essentially a compilation of statistical techniques for the analysis of distribution and for the analysis of factors contributing to those distributions. A primary example of archaeological application is Green's (1973) study of Maya settlement in British Honduras. She used techniques suggested in Haggett to analyze one of the major determinants of settlement, environmental resources, within a framework of optimization of location relative to critical resources. She succeeded in demonstrating a correlation of sites with resources and also suggested the relative importance of these resources. Currently, studies are being undertaken in archaeology with locational analysis as the underlying theme for whole regional studies (Gumerman 1971). One major question is asked: Why do people locate themselves where they do? Archaeology is also beginning to borrow models directly from geography to apply to archaeological data. Currently the most popular is Central Place Theory. Marcus (1973) attempted to use CPT in analyzing the territorial organization of the Classic Lowland Maya. Willey, in his Viru Valley retrospective, suggests that if he had the analysis to do over again, he would also apply Central Place Theory to the settlement study. Other models are available and have been used with some success on archaeological data (see Ucko, Tringham, and Dimbleby 1972 for numerous examples). Models exist to aid in the analysis of all levels of settlement that Trigger (1968) suggests, from models for the individual structure (Rapoport 1969) to diffusion and network models for urban settlements (Hagerstrand 1957; Morrill 1965; Brown 1968). Locational geographers have even studied locational behavior on the individual human level (Pred 1967, 1969) and environmental perception in regard to location (Lowenthal 1967).

These recent applications of geographical techniques to

archaeological problems demonstrate that many archaeologists have come to share Plog's (1968:6-7) view that "... the techniques developed by geographers are directly related to problems of settlement pattern. I believe that anthropologists should take advantage of already proven methods which are applicable to the problems with which they are working." Recent literature in archaeology suggests that direct applications are being made (Washburn 1972, 1974; Green 1973; Marcus 1973). Further, a symposium at the 1974 annual meeting of the Society for American Archaeology was entitled "Central Place Theory and Other Locational Models in Archaeology." Most of these reports and papers, with the exception of Washburn's (1972), were problem-oriented applications of particular geographic techniques. Little concern was given to the general theoretical constructs underlying the techniques. These constructs govern the efficacy of application of a particular technique to a data set and the utility of inferences drawn from results. Such constructs must be carefully considered. The major theoretical notions of utility in archaeology are derived from two sources: economic geography and locational theory.

Economic Geography and Locational Theory

Economic geography has traditionally been concerned with spatial distribution and land use patterns. The majority of techniques used in archaeological applications stem from this source; the most noteworthy technique is the analysis of Central Place. Models developed in economic geography are essentially normative in that they deal with idealized patterns rather than actual spatial organization of economic phenomena. This view is congruent with Hole and Heizer's (1973) characterizations of locational models in geography discussed earlier. This normative approach has not gone uncriticized by geographers.

The major criticisms levied against the normative approach have focused upon its simplicity. Models in economic geography did not account for the multiplicity of factors that influence spatial organization (Harvey 1969:369). Further, economic geographers "... failed or refused to regard any spatial distributions or array of economic features on the landscape as the aggregate reflection of individual decisions" (Pred 1967:11). These arguments reflect behaviorist influence, which Pred suggests was only considered implicitly. Economic geographers tended to accept the generalizations of the environmental determinists and their successors (Pred 1967:11). Little direct attention was paid to the behavioral component of spatial distribution. In recent years, economic geographers have realized that behavioral concepts must be introduced into their models. Some of the criticisms above can be levied against the archaeologist who applies models from economic geography without bearing in mind their normative nature and general lack of behavioral components.

Locational theorists were concerned primarily with behavioral components of spatial distribution in terms of "economic man" models derived from economics, especially the optimizing models of Von Neumann and Morgenstern (1953). The optimizing models of human behavior proposed an "economic man," an omniscient, totally rational construct endowed with perfect predictive powers. One goal, that of maximization, guided behavior. Optimizer strategies were those geared to reap maximum benefits from "best"-choice decisions. Two primary examples demonstrate the limited effectiveness of the model.

Davenport (1960) developed a zero-sum game theory framework to study the fishing-pot locations selected by 26 Jamaican fishermen. If fishing captains placed their pots near shore, they consistently caught sufficient quantities of poor quality fish. If, on the other hand, they placed their pots out to sea, they risked either catching no fish at all as strong currents washed away their pots, or catching sizable quantities of high quality fish if there were no strong current. Davenport wanted to demonstrate an optimizer strategy, and a zero-sum game reveals that an out to sea strategy is the most profitable. A survey of choices indicated that 67% of the fishermen fished near the shore all the time and the remaining 33% mixed their strategies. No fisherman consistently chose the optimal strategy. That no fisherman fished out to sea 100% of the time demonstrates that the optimizer strategy never appeared. Two-thirds selected the prudent strategy of always fishing close to shore even though poor quality was assured.

Gould (1963) chose to use probability theory to predict the planting strategies of farmers in Jantilla, Ghana. Five possible crops were available for planting: cassava, yams, maize, millet, and hill rice. Only maize and hill rice could yield sufficient harvests in both wet and dry years to adequately sustain the population. Gould's research revealed that farmers ignored the substantially larger harvests the other three crops would yield if planted during wet years. They consistently planted maize and rice each year. They did not, therefore, maximize crop production.

The efficacy of the optimizing framework that assumed units involved in decision-making acted ". . . in the guise of 'absolutely rational', 'unerring', economic man" (Pred 1967:11) can be seen from these examples to be minimal. Major criticisms of economic man models in location theory focus on the logical consistency of assumptions of the motives ascribed to economic man, and reject the high level of knowledge and abilities attributed to him. Man often operates in less than optimal ways but usually in ways that satisfy him in terms of needs (Washburn 1972). This satisficing behavior is both culturally and situationally defined.

Pred's (1967, 1969) work suggests that even the satisficing models might not be entirely adequate. When faced with equal options, minimal amounts of information, and limited ability to use the information, man behaves "randomly" or invents *ad hoc* rules by which to rationalize his choices. Pred therefore chose to view locational behavior in terms of real world deviations from the norms provided in both the optimizing and satisficing models. He consequently developed a behavioral matrix to account for variability in decision making.

His behavioral matrix operates through two axes, one a scale of increasing ability to use information, the other a scale of increasing quantity and quality of information. Pred views decisions as adaptive-adoptive. At time 1 (T1), when a decision maker faces a decision with minimal ability to use information and little or no information, his decision will be one that has equal probability with all others of being chosen. If the decision he adopts satisfies his needs, the next time (T2) a decision must be made he has available the information regarding the T1 decision and will adopt that same or at least a similar strategy again. If, on the other hand, his original T1 choice fails to satisfy his needs, he will select a different opinion from the matrix. Given the information about the inferior T1 strategy, he will choose either a slightly or vastly different option from the matrix at T2. The probability that a more satisficing strategy will be selected increases; he thereby adapts. At Tn he will select an optimal, though rarely achieved, strategy. What Pred's matrix allows that the optimizer and satisficer models do not is the input of random factors, changing abilities to make decisions, and ways to account for real world deviations from "normal" behavior.

Consideration of human location in these terms is much like that stated in the introduction to this chapter. These more realistic and less normative models bridge the gap between the approaches to human location that Hole and Heizer (1973) suggest are characteristic of archaeology and geography. Realistic behaviors can be considered, random factors can be included, and specific problems or data sets can be examined within an adaptive

14

framework. In spite of the utility of these approaches to location, translation of general models developed in other disciplines to particular archaeological problems presents further difficulties.

Application of all the locational models discussed above have been relatively easier in geography than in archaeology. Generally, geographic problems have considered living, usually Western, cultures. Therefore, they usually have abundant data and can meet the criteria that Hagerstrand (1952:4) suggests for adequate implementation of most geographic models:

1) Data must be complete and capable of quantitative analysis.
2) Completeness of data must not be restricted to one moment only.
3) Moments should succeed each other at short intervals to give a good idea of order and continuity in the processes under consideration.

In archaeology, the data are generally incomplete and rarely adequate for one moment in time let alone for short intervals that allow any real conceptualization of the processes to be dealt with. Archaeological concerns with locational behavior processes overlap those of the geographer. Archaeology, however, falls short when comparing adequacies of data sets necessary for analysis of the complex variables involved in locational behavior and their relationships.

Archaeological locational problems can best be considered in two ways. Precise relationships between pertinent locational variables can often be determined by the application of hueristic statistical techniques. These techniques are similar to those suggested in Haggett (1965) for geography and applied in archaeology by Green (1973) and Washburn (1974). If the data are adequate and temporal control is otherwise available, the key variables in locational behavior and their interactions can be demonstrated. Selection of variables to be considered is either intuitive or simply reflects prior assumptions about the determination of location. Processes or relationships in statistical form are often difficult to visualize if one is unfamiliar with statistical usage. The degree of contribution of each of the variables is often unclear. Even with adequate data the result can be confusing; with poor data the picture can be even more out of focus. But an alternative approach to locational problems can be used, even when data sets are not adequate for meaningful statistical evaluation, and the relationships and processes are no more difficult to conceptualize than those of statistics.

This alternative approach is the construction of models. Model building can begin with relatively little data at hand. Relevant variables to the locational problem can be intuitively generated or drawn from existing models. The variable relationships can then be deduced. Ultimately, the model can be tested by comparison of a real data set, however weak, to the implied data generated by the hypotheses. The model of particular utility for long-term relationships and processes is a simular model in which the precision of the data is not critical. The processes and hypothesized relationships that have been structured are, however, paramount to the success of the model.

In actuality, the statistical approach and the model building approach are complementary and circular. The inductive methods of the hueristic statistical procedures can generate precise, realistic hypothetical structures to build hypothetico-deductive models. Intuition need not play a key role. If, however, data are not available or easily accessible, they must be generated. This can be accomplished with simular modelling.

The model building approach was selected for use here. The inadequate data available from the Glenwood locality and the complexity of locational behavior demand it. Before considering the Glenwood locational problem itself, the processes and rationales for simular model selection and building must be examined to understand their later application.

2.   The Modelling Process

Relatively few social scientists today work without reference to a model to investigate some phenomenon or set of phenomena (Abler, Adams, and Gould 1971:45). The term model has therefore come to be viewed as a methodological panacea covering a broad spectrum of scientific investigative problems and has, in itself, lost any specific meaning it might once have had. Each individual's specifications for models become imperative to the understanding of his particular research. In the broadest sense, models are hueristic devices, a segment of the scientific method that does not deny the use of imagination or intuition, but seeks to enhance them by controlled use in order to differentiate between mere science fiction and adequate scientific theory (Harvey 1969:292). As Clarke (1972:1-2) suggests:

> Models are pieces of machinery that relate observations to theoretical ideas, they may be used for many different purposes, and they may vary widely in the form of machinery they employ, the class of observations they focus on, and the manner in which they relate the observations to the theory or hypothesis.

Models are partial representations that simplify complex observations by selectively eliminating those details deemed by the investigator as incidental to the phenomenon being investigated. Models isolate essential factors and their interrelationships in such a way as to satisfactorily account for the variability in the observed reality. Their partial nature is to be stressed; a model that attempts to include all the factors potentially relevant to a problem becomes little different from the reality being investigated. Understanding of a causal process, for instance, is best achieved when the variability under investigation is accounted for with the least number of factors and as little noise as possible (cf. Dutton and Starbuck 1971:4). Just as an observer cannot perceive all the variability in any segment of reality, neither can a model incorporate enough factors to account for all the variability. No one model, therefore, can be the simple answer to any problem. Modelling is a basic function of humans that allows them to build the cognitive maps through which they operate;

further, it is basic to the scientific method. Clarke (1972:3) demonstrates the importance of the modelling process to archaeology and other disciplines:

Why need the archeologist concern himself with models? There are five main reasons, which may be briefly outlined:

1) Whether we appreciate it or not our personal archeological opinions, approach, aims and selection of projects are *controlled* by largely subconscious mind models which we accumulate through time. We should realize that we are thus controlled.

2) Whether we appreciate it or not we always operate conceptual models in the interpretation of observations. We all resemble the Moliere character who was delighted to find that all his life, unknowingly, he had been speaking prose. We should make these operational models explicit and testable.

3) The construction, testing, verification or refutation and modification of explicit models is the essence of the empirical and scientific approaches—providing the progressive cycle by means of which fresh information and insight are gained and theory is accumulated. Observations, hypothesis, experiment, conclusions, fresh hypothesis, fresh observations. . . .

4) The existence of a model presupposes the existence of an underlying theory, since a model is but one simplified, formalized and skeletal expression of a theory—be it tacit or explicit—developed for a particular situation. A careful study of groups of models apparently expressing a common underlying theory for different situations may therefore help us to expose, and articulate latent theory in a palpable and widely powerful form (Harvey 1969:146-7). Model definition is a route to the explicit theory which essentially defines a vigorous discipline.

5) Finally: Hypotheses are generated from the model expression of a theory.
Explanation comes from tested hypotheses.
Hypotheses are tested by using relevant analyses on meaningful categories of data.

Within the generalized definition of model many different specific types of models are feasible, be they descriptive (visualizing), organizing (taxonomic), or explanatory in function. A number of attempts have been made to categorize models on the basis of form and function (Rosenbluth and Weiner 1945; Churchman, Ackoff, and Arnoff 1957; Sayre and Crosson 1963; Haggett and Chorley 1967; Harvey 1969; Clarke 1972). The most exacting and inclusive taxonomy to date has been presented by Mihram (1972a). His taxonomy is heavily relied on for the discussion below and his table of exemplary models is presented in slightly altered form in Table 1.

Table 1. *Exemplary Models*

	Material		Analogue	Descriptive	Symbolic	
	Replication	Quasi-replica			Simular	Formalization
STATIC Deterministic	Earthen Relief Map	Road Map	Statue of B. Franklin	Ten Commandments	Decision Logic Tables	Ohm's Law
Stochastic	Critical Dosage Test	Weather Map	Die Toss for Russian Roulette	Weather Report	Non-Adaptive, Random, Chess Playing Program	Equilibrium Queue Length
DYNAMIC Deterministic	Model Train Set	Planetarium Show	Analog Computer Circuitry for $y = -y$	Constitution of U.S.A.	Critical Path Algorithm	Lanchester's Laws
Stochastic	Drosophila Genetic Experiment	CRT Display of Endurance Test	White Noise Generator	Text on Darwinian Evolution	Vehicle-By-Vehicle Transportation Model	Stochastic Differential Equation

Increasing Abstraction ⟶
Increasing Inferential Facility
Decreased Reality

Increasing Generality ⟶

(After Mihram 1972a:624)

As one moves from the upper left hand corner to the lower right hand corner of Table 1, the models increase in both generality and abstraction, concomitantly decreasing in inferential facility and degree of reality. Such variability in type often causes difficulties in the selection and implementation of a particular kind of model for a particular kind of problem. Replicas of phenomena require no drastic change of medium from the modelled phenomena to the model itself and are quite easily understood by the user. On the other hand, symbolic or analogue models require a relatively major change of medium causing some loss of facility in understanding and implementation. Consider, for instance, the differences between the earthlodge burning model constructed by Smith (1953) and the Markov chain model used by Thomas (1972).

As suggested earlier, the model building procedure is akin to the scientific method. Mihram (1972a:625) identifies six stages in the procedure (Fig. 1). Before any model is constructed, it is imperative that the designer considers what the specific goals of the model are to be; that is, what are the appropriate measures of the performance of the system? This stage, *Model Goals*, is elemental in the later selection of the variety of model to be used. Once the selection is made, the salient components of the system being modelled, their interactions and relationships, and the system's dynamic behavior mechanics are isolated in the *Systems Analysis* stage. *System Synthesis* is comprised of organizing the system's behavior in accordance with the systems analysis stage. The model's responses are then compared in the *Verification* stage with those responses that would be anticipated if the model's structure was indeed prepared as intended. The responses resulting from the verified model are then compared with the observations of and measurements from the real system. This is an effort at *Validation*. The final stage, *Inference*, is concerned with the definition of experiments with and comparisons of responses from the verified and validated models. The process is essentially cyclical; at any stage, one can drop back to an earlier stage if problems are encountered. If the results produced by the model are deemed inadequate, the only assumptions remaining are that the system being modelled is behaving in such a complex and irrational way due to incomprehensible forces, or that the model as constructed is simply inadequate (Morrill 1965:14). If the latter is determined to be the difficulty, the only solution is a return to an earlier stage in the modelling process.

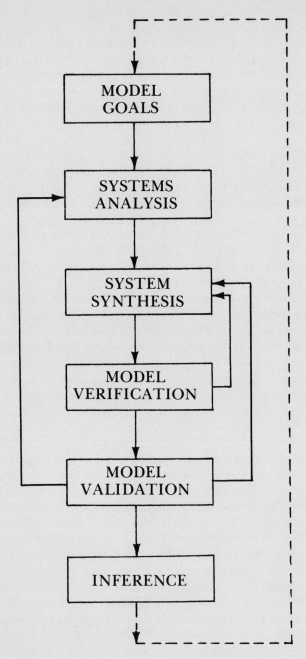

Fig. 1. *The Modelling Process*

Systems Analysis

A system is comprised of a number of constituent elements and the intrinsic mechanisms that relate those elements to each other. Therefore, the first stage in the analysis of the system to be modelled is the breaking down of the system into its component entities. The analyst is immediately confronted with the difficulty of deciding whether certain elements contribute to the system's behavior or whether they are simply a part of the system's environment. The sorting of elements is accomplished "by exiling to the environment those elements which, though they may from time to time affect system entities significantly, are never affected significantly by any of the elements (entities) intrinsic to the system" (Mihram 1972a:626). Other elements included in the environment are those that, even though affected significantly by elements definitely intrinsic to the system, do not in turn affect system elements. For example, in dealing with a cultural system, elements such as climatic factors might fall into the former category while topography or geomorphology might fall into the latter. In essence, it appears that this sorting process involves seeking out the various feedback mechanisms of the system. The primary goals of this stage, then, include the delineation of the components of the system that interact with each other as the system moves through time, and the demarcation or assignment of system boundaries that allow conceptualization of the system and the environment in which it operates.

While the system entities are being defined, the analyst should further determine the necessary attributes of each entity. In this way, the state variables, which allow monitoring of the system's status at any point in time, can be tabulated. The analyst further defines the mechanisms by which state variables change, whether by instantaneous events (e.g., births) or continuous flow events (e.g., tidewater fluctuations). It would seem that some systems could be modelled with both types of changes included and that the analyst's conceptualization of the modelled phenomenon basically determines variety of change. In any case, it is necessary that the state variable change mechanisms be understood or defined.

One proceeds in analysis in much the same fashion as "top-down" programming or flow charting in which the entities and feedback situations are at first very broadly defined. Diligent examination of these broadly stated elements and behavioral aspects usually leads to an understanding of the hierarchical nature of the system; that is, elements defined originally might be viewed as comprised of one or more lower level subsystems with components and behavioral aspects of their own. The result of reiterated examination of the model at lower levels eventually leads to a general uncertainty concerning the subsystems and their interactions, especially their synergetic impact on the higher levels. Due to the limitations of available information (data) and increased cost in terms of time, certain potentially knowable subsystems must be viewed as contributing in random ways to the system being modelled. Thus, realistic models can never be deterministic; realistic models that are conscientiously developed eventuate a requirement for stochasticity (Mihram 1972a:626).

Once matters of system boundaries, environment, entities, attributes, and feedback mechanisms have been delineated, the systems analysis stage is essentially completed. This is the most difficult developmental stage in the modelling process and perhaps involves the greatest amount of subjectivity in decisions on the part of the analyst.

System Synthesis

Synthesis of the system is essentially concerned with physically structuring and implementing the model. Since much of the model structuring has been considered in the systems analysis stage, the major task of synthesis is the determination of the variety of model to be used. If a dynamic model is selected, the next decision is whether to make the model deterministic or stochastic. As suggested in the discussion of systems analysis, a number of seemingly random factors may be operating (based either on truly random operation or simply uncertainty of system behavior). A stochastic model will probably be necessary and, in fact, will probably give more realistic, believable results. Should system behavior be recognized to follow well-defined, logical operations, then a deterministic model would perhaps be more efficient. Some models will, in different levels of the system, include both. Inclusion of either determinism or stochasticism for its own sake is inadequate (Mihram 1972a:627).

The choice between the various material or symbolic models is also relatively important. Material models that permit greater visualizing capabilities often allow less control over changes in state variables that would perhaps facilitate verification and validation of the model. Symbolic models, on the other hand, allow control and ease in the handling of a large number of variables. The ultimate decision is eventually one of cost analysis, especially in matters of accuracy, data requirements, and flexibility for experimentation.

After model selection, the next major synthetic task is construction of the model prototype. In the case of static and dynamic material models, this means building the physical components of the model; for dynamic symbolic models, it often means selection of a computer language and programming in that language.

Verification

For models, the verification stage consists of locating any logical faults in the model's structure. For computerized models, this stage is essentially one of debugging the program built in the synthesis stage and performing calibration tests on it. Material models present certain difficulties inherent in the nature of the media selected for construction; verification must often come through visual means by comparison to the modelled phenomenon, and must usually be carried out during the synthesis stage. Dynamic models (either material or symbolic) should, at the end of T units of time, yield a response R(T), which may be represented as a function of input or environmental conditions parameterized as a vector $(x_1, x_2, \ldots, x_p)$, with the response becoming

$$R(T) = r_T(x_1, x_2, \ldots, x_p).$$

For stochastic models, the response is a random variable

$$R(T) = R_T(x_1, x_2, \ldots, x_p; S)$$

$$= r_T(x_1, x_2, \ldots, x_p) + e(S)$$

where $r_T(x_1, x_2, \ldots, x_p)$ is a generally known response function representing the expected model response at environmental specification $(x_1, x_2, \ldots, x_p)$. The random variable $e(S)$ has mean zero and is a transformation of the randomly selected seed number S as required explicitly by most stochastic computerized models (see Mihram 1972a:627 for a more complete discussion).

In deterministic models, the response is a function of the specific environmental conditions and could be precisely predicted given proper logical structuring of the model. For stochastic models, verification requires statistical procedures. Given that the model depends on probabilistic functions, the verification tests for stochastic models might fail even though the model is properly structured. These tests are often construed as tests of the model's random number generator (Mihram 1972a:627). In the case of both deterministic and stochastic models, verification is carried out not by comparison of the model's response with responses of the system being modelled, but rather by comparison of the model's response with theoretically anticipated results in as many cases as possible. Again, the intent of verification is to check the logical consistency of the model to determine whether the model is behaving as the modeller expected.

Validation

Validation of a model occurs when responses from a verified model and the actual system are compared to see how well the responses or measurements correspond with each other. Given that such tests are ready to be made, the operating conditions are fixed for the actual system; after T time units, the results are recorded. The corresponding environmental conditions are set for the model, and after comparable time has elapsed, the results are recorded and compared on a one-to-one basis with the responses from the modelled system. Such an approach assumes that the actual system is available for manipulation. In many instances (especially man related phenomena) that system is not available; when this is so, optimal validation procedures are not feasible. Any inferences drawn from such circumstances are simply made at greater risk.

A number of established procedures for validation are available (Efron 1971; Sage and Melsa 1971; Mihram 1972b). For deterministic models, the comparisons are rather easily made. Variation or discrepancy between model and modelled responses indicates that the systems analysis stage was improperly carried out and that the stages of analysis, synthesis, and verification must be reiterated. Validation, like verification, is a statistical matter in stochastic models. Multiple "runs" of the model need to be compared with the real system and such criteria as equality of means and homogeneity of variance need to be applied. Failure of performance, therefore, is often a subjective matter, especially in extremely complex models. Further, output is often so complex that statistical validation is difficult to conduct, and multiple "runs" tend to be costly in terms of both time and funds. Unacceptable performance again implies some error at the initial stages of model development.

Inference

Inference from a model's construction and performance falls into a tenuous realm of manipulation of the validated model. Experimentation can be carried on pursuing several lines of inquiry. Given validated behavior during a set number of temporal units, the question is asked as to the system's behavior over a greater span of time. What effects are evident on the environmental conditions over that time, or what impact does a planned change in environmental conditions have? Finally, what particular set of environmental conditions can be specified to promote a situation in which the model's response is in some way optimized? This inferential stage is likened to "play" with the model. The results of this "play" are often so profound and totally unexpected that the experimenter is allowed new insight into the system's behavior that revolutionizes his thinking. Thomas (1971) likens this situation to serendipity.

Summary

The stages of goal selection, systems analysis, synthesis, verification, validation, and inference involved in the modelling process are cyclical in nature, not unlike the procedures of the scientific method. As such, the process becomes a means of control for an individual and his intuitions, but at the same time allows enough flexibility so that as great a spectrum of insight as possible into phenomena under investigation can be gained.

In the investigation of particularly complex phenomena, such controlled procedures facilitate research by imposing logic on the analysis of systems and testing of models. Phenomena with a few well understood variables can be considered within the framework of a more deterministic model. Phenomena with multiple networks of functionally and temporally linked components are somewhat more intractable and can perhaps best be investigated using a model of the dynamic, stochastic, simular form. Such a form could be especially beneficial for the study of complex human behavioral phenomena. As Mihram (1972a:625) suggests, a simular model ". . . frequently provides just the appropriate balance of realism, ease of experimentation, cost of model maintenance, accuracy and stability that one seeks."

3. Simulation of Human Behavioral Phenomena

Simulation has been going on since man first developed the brainpower to imagine. "The child with a doll, the architect with a model, and the businessman with a plan are all simulating" (McLeod 1968:1). It is little wonder that "simulation" has become as confused in its definition as "model." Simulation does mean different things to different people, but in general is considered to mean "the act of representing some aspects of the real world by numbers or symbols which may be easily manipulated to facilitate their study" (McLeod 1968:4). This definition sounds very much like the definition of model offered earlier, especially when expanded to include ". . . the development and use of models for the study of the dynamics of existing and hypothetical systems" (Brennan 1968:5). Confusion is not altogether allayed by Mihram (1972a:632) whose use of the term "simular" includes "those symbolic models whose component symbols are not entirely manipulated by the operations of well formed disciplines such as mathematics, mathematical logic, or numerical analysis." (Examples would be an algorithmic food recipe, a static and deterministic simular model; or a computer program that describes the passenger by passenger emptying and loading of a city bus along its route, a dynamic and stochastic simular model.) In other words, simulations can simply be regarded as one possible dimension of a variety of model types. They are simple representations of reality that are manipulated in accordance with the dicta of the investigator constructing the model. We are not unlike a child playing with a doll; we learn from the simulation about phenomena under investigation much as the child learns from doll play about interpersonal relationships or family life. We do not learn all about reality, but interact with reality via our "toy" in a way that will better facilitate our comprehension of, and give us at least a flavor of, the real thing.

The Nature of Simulation: Advantages and Disadvantages

The process of simulation encompasses the design and study of a model of a system; motivations for its use come from a number of sources. As an abstract model becomes less abstract and general and more realistic and specific, it also becomes more intractable mathematically. "We cannot easily determine the behavior of systems whose variables are discontinuous, stochastic, and intimately related to many other such variables in a multiplicative fashion" (Wyman 1970:1). We do witness such complexity in the real world and can often best comprehend complexity only if we deal with it in as realistic a fashion as possible. Consequently, "simulation's most prominent attractions are intelligible results and freedom from the constraints of mathematical ignorance" (Dutton and Starbuck 1971:4). The implications of relationships that are nonlinear or irregular in some other fashion can be explored without restriction to some mathematically convenient assumptions. Simulation does, however, impose some degree of logical rigor on an investigator by causing him to analyze the temporal structure of modelled processes or systems. For computer simulations this quality is inherent in that no output will be produced if assumptions are not logically structured. If an investigator builds an operating program, he is forced to consider temporal sequence or to specify which operation comes before which other operation. In this way he moves toward a comprehension of causality. Simulation is a particularly useful technique when the real system or situation under consideration is not available for direct manipulation. The extension of a model of an operating system through time is useful as a predictive device, but without the real system, inferences drawn from the model remain hypothetical. The inferences are only as adequate as any underlying assumptions concerning real system environment or operations.

Those instances where simulation can be usefully employed even though the real system is not available pinpoint the greatest disadvantages of simulation. Even though the simulator has too little information to specify the relational and temporal assumptions to be incorporated into his model, he is required to specify them in very precise ways. Consequently, he is often induced to substitute conjecture or speculation for investigation and fact. Further, the computer languages used in simulation often vary in their facility such that even with precise adequate information, the conceptual structures of the simulator cannot be realized in the program. Finally, the search for realistic forms of output can overshadow the need for realistic associations between the input and the output. All in all, the simulator is faced with major problems whenever he attempts to create a realistic simular model.

The quest for realism in an extreme form can lead to what has been labelled "Bonini's Paradox" (Bonini 1963:136) or the complexity dilemma. Simular models are constructed such that assumptions and functional relations may be as complex or realistic as possible so that some observed causal process can be better understood. The outputs of the model will likely resemble reality in such a way that the model will be deemed an accurate representation of the real process. But, with the model's complex set of assumptions and their relations, the simulation is no easier to understand than the real process. If the researcher "... hopes to understand complex behavior, he must construct complex models, but the more complex the model, the harder it is to understand" (Dutton and Briggs 1971:103). Since the purpose of science is to make things simpler, constructing a model as, or more, complex than reality is self-defeating.

Simulation, then, as the controlled manipulation of symbols representing a real system, is a means by which an investigator can study any particular system without actually manipulating the system itself. Its goal remains an understanding of some causal process. Simulation allows the application of a rather rigorous logical framework to an extremely complex situation that is either difficult or impossible to analyze mathematically. Consequently, the use of simulation to analyze an extremely complex system such as the behavior of total societies, which is often considered too complex to analyze quantitatively, might seem a reasonable step.

Simulation of Behavior of Total Societies

Dutton and Briggs (1971:103) define a simulation of behavior in terms of conditions that must be satisfied. A simulation should: 1) examine a behavior process; 2) give a theory or model that describes and explains the process without ambiguity; 3) show how the process is affected by its environment; and 4) be formulated in such a way that inferences about the process may be verified by observation. Behavior process is defined as an activity that undergoes transformation through time, depending partly on the initial state of the environment and the subsequent response to that environment by the activity. The activity may both operate on its environment and be determined by its environment. The Dutton and Briggs view of behavior is essentially systemic and fits well within the framework for models discussed earlier. Their conditions could be a synonymous definition for most dynamic models. Simulations of behavior processes have been executed effectively for relatively low level human phenomena, particularly in psychology and business management (Starbuck and Dutton 1971:31-102), but few have dealt effectively with the broader behavioral phenomena of human aggregates.

The reason for this relative paucity of broader behavioral simulations is simply this: it is perhaps possible to study a total society but it is impossible to study a total society totally (Pool 1967:45). There is no such thing as a complete description of even the smallest event, let alone a complete description of a total society. As an investigator, one must select from the infinite range of alternative good descriptions. Consequently, there is the possibility for an infinite number of problems to be solved and an infinite number of solutions to each of those problems. Seeking an absolutely correct single solution to a problem has led to frustration and confusion. If even at the lowest levels the frustration and confusion exist, how much greater it must be for individuals working at higher and more complex behavioral levels. The result has been few relatively high level simulations of total societies.

The strictures of missing data or "infinite" data have been suggested as a rationale for ignoring total societies (a suggestion that would hurt anthropology dearly) and abandoning simulation, which requires such precise information for the structuring of models. The question simply becomes a matter of ambiguity or precision. However, a simulation may be more useful than its data (Pool 1967:57). The value of a simulation lies as much or more in the study of process as in the measures of particular real world parameter values. If the mechanisms by which a process operates are understood or at least hypothesized by an investigator, they can still be structured for simulation. For the data necessary to the system's environment or operations, parameter estimations or simply arbitrary figures can be used. The results will probably be an incorrect solution for the particular real world problem, but the hypothesized structure of a process will be examinable. Perhaps comparing the real system results with the results derived from the estimated parameters, together with understanding the process, generates means for more precisely estimating the real problem data. Simulation in this instance becomes an ever more specific and accurate cyclical procedure.

Given the limitations of the study of total societies discussed earlier, the best that can be hoped for is a simulation representing one or a few aspects of a society, but never all aspects. Those simulations done in geography concerning diffusion of innovation (e.g., Hagerstrand 1952, 1957) have considered such aspects of society as social networks and media dissemination of information. In anthropology, simulations have been concerned with population dynamics (e.g., Dyke and MacCluer 1974) or kinship (e.g., Gilbert and Hammel 1966); for archaeology specifically, relatively few simulations have been done and only two have been published that are directly concerned with settlement. These simulations (Thomas 1971, 1972, 1973, 1974; Zubrow 1971a, 1971b) will be examined briefly below.

Simulation of Prehistoric Settlement Patterns

The application of computer simulation techniques to any sort of archaeological situation is perhaps one of the newest uses of the computer for archaeology. That Whallon (1972:37-38) devotes little more than half a page to a discussion of simulation is an indication of its relatively new status in the discipline. He expresses wonder at the situation when he says, "the techniques and procedures of computer simulation so closely parallel the current thinking and processes of model building of many archaeologists that the lateness and limits of their application are surprising" (Whallon 1972:38). He cites as reasons those factors already discussed above, but in particular notes the difficulty of establishing the necessary accurate parameters and variables from archaeological data. Even though simulation was proposed as a potentially valuable tool for anthropologists as early as 1965 (Hays 1965), it should be noted that it was not suggested for use in archaeology in any detailed way until 1970 (Doran 1970). Explanation for this lag is perhaps related to the development of applications of a systems approach. Computer simulations are so akin to systems models that understanding of the use of systems models can be seen as a prerequisite to the use of simulation. As it now stands, computer simulation remains one of the few ways to adequately test a systems model. Systems theoretical frameworks have only recently been applied; consequently, few simulations have been operationalized. Only two writers (Thomas 1971, 1972, 1973, 1974; Zubrow 1971a, 1971b) deal effectively with settlement patterning, but both are focused primarily on aspects other than settlement and the locational process.

Zubrow's (1971a, 1971b) major concern was the generation and operationalization of a model of environmental carrying capacity as a dynamic equilibrating system. He used the Neo-Malthusian concept that population continues to increase up to the carrying capacity and then stabilizes. Dealing with the impact of population pressure within a series of organized, spatially differentiated ecosystems in the Hay Hollow Valley of Arizona between A.D. 300 and A.D. 1400, he developed a simular model using FORTRAN IV. Realizing that more elements than population and resources interacted, he incorporated variables of time, space, technology, climate, migration, and settlement patterning into his model. The model used was essentially deterministic with constant resource availability assumed (or known to decrease ca. A.D. 1150) for the valley during the 1100 year time span; rates of population growth were contingent on the resource base. The most intriguing segment of the model dealt with locational behavior in regard to population pressure on the carrying capacity.

Zubrow hypothesized that if a population overshoots the carrying capacity by a simple growth or immigration, the population would ultimately die out or leave the area. Growth would begin in the optimal resource zones, and as population spread to the marginal zones, the process would be repeated with each marginal zone having a smaller carrying capacity. His tests from Hay Hollow Valley generally supported this hypothesis that population development in marginal zones was a function of optimal zone exploitation. He further suggested the interaction of the underlying variables that would allow the hypothesis to be operationalized. Settlement attributes such as population aggregation, spatial aggregation, and residential area were considered. Zubrow offered that if population density was at or exceeding carrying capacity as available resources began to drop, the smaller villages would depopulate first due to an insufficient manpower base to continue subsistence, religion, and political activites. Thus the smaller populations would migrate to other villages or out of the area. During resource depletion, then, population aggregation occurs; as resources decrease there will be fewer sites but relatively more individuals per site. In support of this notion, Zubrow observed that the number of rooms in smaller sites decreases or remains the same. As the population aggregates, spatial aggregation also occurs as a result of the increasing necessity for the population to use areas of optimal resource production during periods of resource depletion (Zubrow 1971a:279). A nearest neighbor index of spatial dispersion and aggregation on the Hay Hollow Valley data revealed increased spatial aggregation. In terms of residential area, Zubrow suggested that since more of a population would be involved in priority subsistence tasks, fewer people would be involved in construction of large residential structures. Again, his data indicated that such was the case since there was a concomitant decrease in residential area as resources decreased.

In all, Zubrow's is a generalized systemic model that deals peripherally with locational problems. His use of population as a causal factor exemplifies suggestions of Smith (1972) in terms of the role of population pressure in archaeological explanation. Certain of his concepts concerning population aggregations will be used in the problem presented here.

Thomas (1971, 1972, 1973, 1974) developed a function specific model designed to simulate deposition of artifacts resulting from the ethnographic subsistence pattern of the Shoshone of the Great Basin as posited by Steward (1941). The model focused on the seasonal rounds in Shoshonean subsistence activities and particularly on a number of procurement subsystems. Thomas's model, as opposed to Zubrow's, was considerably more stochastic. Given the hypothesized stability of the generalized Shoshone hunting and gathering system, he reasoned that the model would have essentially performed the same task over the thousand year period and would thus have accounted for little variability in terms of actual artifact distribution. Therefore, in his FORTRAN IV-based BASIN I simulation program, he used variable input from the system's environment as the model's probabilistic core.

Thomas's technique was to examine the year by year variation of resource availability in terms of the variable productivity of potential food items, especially pinyon nuts, ricegrass, and pronghorn antelope. He calculated the probabilities of success in gathering adequate yearly crops of nuts and other food items. These probabilities were stated in the form of Markov chains and were used as Monte Carlo, i.e., random number, input into the transition matrices. In this way, Thomas derived predictions as to the availability of adequate crops in the following year given the current year's productivity. Thus, the likelihood of groups exploiting a particular resource zone could be predicted.

Thomas also subdivided the artifact assemblages he was considering into three major functional groups: a hunting assemblage consisting strictly of stone projectile points; a plant procurement assemblage consisting mainly of a seed knife; and a habitation group assemblage consisting of dwellings, artifacts for food preparation or preservation, items for tool manufacture and repairs, and items for clothing manufacture and repair. The hypothesized deposition of those artifacts he expressed in terms of density; that is, each resource zone should contain more of one kind of artifact assemblage than the other zones (e.g., the greatest density of pinyon processing artifacts would be in the pinyon-juniper zone). His predictions were also phrased in terms of distribution, using a Coefficient of Dispersion. For example, hunting artifacts are expected to be relatively random in their distribution while dwellings should be relatively nucleated. For the 1000 year run of the simulation, BASIN I predicted 48 Coefficients of Dispersion and 66 relating to density (Thomas 1973:171).

Thomas used surface and excavated data from the Reese River Valley of Nevada to test the predictions of the simulations. Over all, 86% of the quantitative predictions were verified (Thomas 1973:171). Therefore, it would seem that the Shoshonean settlement/subsistence pattern as simulated was much like the real pattern as indicated in the archaeological record of the Reese River Valley. In all, the settlement pattern in the valley was characterized by summer camps near the river shoreline. The pattern was focused on the permanent water source and the summer-ripened grass and root crops. Winter camps were in the pinyon ecotone and focused on the pinyon nut supplemented by hunting. Thomas (1973:173) labeled the pattern as dual central base wandering.

The stochastic simulation techniques used by Thomas made the BASIN I model considerably more realistic and specific than Zubrow's Hay Hollow Valley model. The major difference was in intent; Thomas's model was for specific hypothesis testing, whereas Zubrow's was for determing the general interaction of two variables, carrying capacity and population. Both were successful in indicating to some extent the nature of locational processes in two different prehistoric groups. Their approaches seem useful for testing models that have been developed earlier, as in Thomas's case, or for generating new explanations. Their works provide examples for the development of a simular model to account for changing settlement in the Glenwood locality.

4. Changing Concepts of Settlement Patterns in the Glenwood Locality

Although mention of settlement had been made in earlier reports of Central Plains tradition localities (Gilder 1911:252; Strong 1935:263; Hill and Cooper 1936:217), the sense of these discussions was generally locatory. That is, the question was simply where the settlements were situated on the landscape. After Willey's (1953) Viru Valley settlement analysis, the substance of discussions on settlement changed. Emphasis shifted from location alone to the delineation of patterning as well as interpretation of those patterns in a context of cultural ecology. Wedel's (1956) paper, "Changing Settlement Patterns in the Great Plains," considered Central Plains tradition settlement in those terms, and his later (Wedel 1959, 1961) analyses became the usually accepted description of the tradition. His statements have only recently come under major criticism (Gradwohl 1969).

Nebraska Phase Settlement

Wedel (1961:95) analyzed Nebraska phase settlement and reconstructed a dispersed pattern:

> Villages show little or no evidence of planning. In the Nebraska culture they consisted of house units strung irregularly along the tops of ridges and bluffs; others may be scattered on lower terraces, where their arrangement is now obscured by slope wash and other factors.

The major reconstructed pattern, then, consisted of small, scattered, isolated houses found usually in linear arrangement on ridgelines or bluffs and occasional small clusters of houses (two to four) found on terraces or hillslopes near small streams.

Gradwohl (1969:135) analyzed the development of this reconstructed pattern and saw it as the result of Wedel's own studies in Kansas and Nebraska and a reflection of work done by Sterns (1914, 1915a, 1915b), Strong (1935), and Cooper (1936, 1939). Gradwohl's own detailed analysis of settlement descriptions and excavation reports led him to conclude that Wedel's pattern was perhaps an artifact of the way archaeologists doing the analyses of settlement data had conceptualized their research.

It is Gradwohl's (1969:1-2) contention ". . . that small nucleated villages were at least one of the settlement patterns of the Nebraska culture, instead of or in addition to . . ." the pattern described by Wedel. The failure of many Plains archaeologists to recognize this is deeply rooted in the history of Plains archaeology. The following are the major points of Gradwohl's (1969:135) arguments. Site units in the Central Plains were initially conceptualized as individual lodges that showed up as surface depressions. These depressions were noted, but when excavation was done, it was only of sites with the superficial indicators. Little effort was made to test areas that did not exhibit obvious signs of a lodge's presence. Several areas that did have a more nucleated pattern were mentioned, but were not published in detail; some larger nucleated villages did exist. Finally, Gradwohl suggests that the theoretical orientation of the Midwestern Taxonomic System, which requires that temporal and spatial dimensions be treated separately from form, was not amenable to the study of settlement in which time and space play integral roles. Due then to the interplay of many factors, the archaeologist was predisposed to accept the usual definition of Central Plains tradition settlement as dispersed; consequently, few efforts have been geared toward discovery of alternative patterns.

Gradwohl's (1969) observations appear to have been confirmed by his own study of settlement patterns in the Weeping Water locality of eastern Nebraska. Few other Nebraska phase localities have come under such close scrutiny. Gradwohl has done much to explain the Nebraska phase settlement patterns and the reasons for inadequate descriptions of that pattern. However, he does not explain the reasons for the variable settlement patterns in other Central Plains tradition localities (Anderson 1961; Wood 1969; Krause 1970). Such variability seems to exist in the Glenwood, Iowa, locality just across the Missouri River from the Weeping Water locality. That variability will be examined here.

Glenwood Locality Settlement

The subject of settlement patterns in the Glenwood locality was first raised by Proudfit (1881) in his reports of surveys and excavations near Glenwood. He reported that the 45 houses he located were normally in small groups associated with burial mounds. He concluded that the people who made the houses had also constructed the mounds (Proudfit 1881:272). He and Dean (1881) also described the cultural debris found in the lodges, especially the ceramics. Their coverage was spotty, and the comments related to settlement were limited to a few lines.

The next major contribution was made in the 1930's by Ellison Orr, who, under the auspices of the State Historical Society of Iowa, conducted an intensive site survey of the Glenwood area. He located 68 houses, only five of which could be positively identified as houses reported by Proudfit (Orr 1963:1). That Orr must have located most of the sites seen by Proudfit seems likely. Orr stresses that his evidence for the settlement pattern was directly opposed to Proudfit's statements. Even allowing for the obliteration of a number of houses during the interval between their studies, most of the lodges could not be considered part of a larger group since 47 of the 68 were separated from their nearest neighbor by more than half a mile (Orr 1963:5). Occupation of the ridgelines perplexed Orr (1963:8), who observed that the houses would have been exposed to the full force of the winter winds, and even though firewood was abundant, the nearest source of water was often more than a quarter of a mile away. He disagreed with Proudfit's suggestion that the Indians had located their lodges with an eye for the view, pointing out that the houses were well back from the bluffline and that trees would have obscured the view (Orr 1963:4, 8).

Orr was also concerned with the length of time involved in the habitation of the locality. If a single large community was represented, the habitation must have been relatively short; if the distribution of the houses was the result of a small community building new houses to replace old, dilapidated ones, the locality might evidence considerable time depth and cultural change (Orr 1963:7).

During the next 20 years, the Glenwood locality materials were classified by Keyes (1951:340) as the Glenwood focus of the Nebraska aspect according to the Midwestern Taxonomic System. He utilized the individual house sites on blufflines as a key trait defining the focus. Little excavation was done during the period and few new house locations were noted. The only excavation was reported by amateurs (Davis and Rowe 1960).

Anderson (1961) became concerned with the time depth problem in the Glenwood locality, a problem that had earlier been discussed by Orr. Anderson's major interest was the development of a local sequence of sites, particularly for the taxonomic reasons associated with applying the Willey-Phillips scheme to the Glenwood materials. He seriated the ceramics from 12 houses excavated by Orr and four houses that he and others had excavated in one of the hollows opening onto the Missouri River floodplain. The four houses were part of what he labeled a village of an estimated 15 houses. If accurate, it is the largest concentration of houses for the locality (Anderson 1961:54). The result of his seriation was a division of the Glenwood local sequence into three phases: Pony Creek, Keg Creek, and Kullbom. Anderson implied that at least three communities existed in the locality that were distinct temporally, formally, and spatially. He also seemed to feel that the development of the communities was a continuum through the three phases.

Brown (1967) excavated a series of lodges in the locality as part of a watershed salvage operation in the Pony Creek drainage. He necessarily concentrated his work in the valleys and adjacent hillslopes affected by construction and located several houses that appear to be part of a small cluster. His work was descriptive, however, and did little except challenge Anderson's three-phase local sequence. Brown proposed two sub-phases and actually reversed the order presented in Anderson's sequence. He too implied a continuous development for the cultural materials in the locality, but did not indicate whether he conceptualized the development as one community through time or several small communities.

Intensive highway and watershed salvage and the excavation of several more lodges began in 1969. These operations are continuing at present. With some of the houses radiocarbon dated, Zimmerman (1971) reanalyzed the local sequence developed by Anderson and contested by Brown, and incorporated new data into a new seriation. Little was resolved concerning the sequence orientation problems discussed in Anderson and Brown. In attempting to orient the sequence or at least to corroborate the temporal position of the dated sites, it was discovered that sites with early dates (ca. A.D. 900) fell between sites with much later dates (ca. A.D. 1200). A number of alternative hypotheses were offered to explain the differences, including a suggestion that a number of small contemporaneous communities existed in the locality at various times during its occupation. Even though the communities shared many basic formal traits, each might have emphasized slightly different traits, causing enough diversity in the ceramic assemblage to foul the seriation. In essence, the problem could have been the result of spatial variation. A shift in focus from single house sites to entire communities was suggested as a different perspective on the development of the ceramic assemblage (Zimmerman 1971:22). This suggestion differed from the approach that Anderson and Brown took in that the development of the Glenwood settlement distribution and formal variation is seen as the result of a single community developing through time.

The Anderson-Zimmerman Model

The various descriptions of settlement distribution in the Glenwood locality offered by Proudfit (1881) and Orr (1963), as well as the perplexing problems of spatial differentiation of cultural forms and their time depth, began to cause confusion over the actual form of settlement in the area. With Gradwohl's (1969) enlargement of the generally accepted settlement for Central Plains tradition, Anderson and Zimmerman (n.d.) chose to examine the known distribution of lodges in the Glenwood locality. They felt that Wedel's descriptions of Central Plains tradition settlement adequately indicated the presence of variations in the patterns (Anderson and Zimmerman n.d.:12). Wedel's (1959:506) composite view of the pattern was felt to be characterized by both the single houses on ridgelines and bluffs and the small loosely organized hamlets or villages located on stream terraces. Small groups of houses occurred "... with usually half a dozen to a score of earth-covered dwellings" (Wedel 1959:506). Wedel's references to the prevalence of individual households and their seemingly random distribution, while a common theme, appeared balanced by references to larger communites. An interest in a form of settlement so different from the later large Plains villages was felt to be the cause of overemphasizing the dispersed pattern or at least deemphasizing the nucleated arrangements. Gradwohl was credited with revitalizing the more complete settlement description. Anderson and Zimmerman chose to consider why the settlement variability existed or at least to assess the significance of its occurrence.

They analyzed the known distribution of lodges in the Glenwood locality according to the framework of settlement determinants outlined by Trigger (1968) in his analysis of individual structures and the distribution of structures within a single community. Using a quasi-systemic framework, a model was presented to account for the variability. Since the Anderson-Zimmerman model is integral to the model built here, it will be briefly discussed.

The original Nebraska phase inhabitants of the locality were viewed as semisedentary, and it was assumed that all or at least part of their annual food procurement cycle could have been carried out within the locality. Residents probably practiced a rather even mixture of hunting, gathering, and horticulture. Analysis of floral and faunal resource zones suggested that distance would not have been a problem in the acquisition of food or in its transport to the lodges for processing since all the resource zones could be accessed within a mile or so of any lodge. No evidence for or against an annual extended hunt was available. There was considerable evidence for horticulture based on the presence of charred fragments of corn and beans together with the bison scapula hoe. It was assumed that a slash-and-burn horticultural pattern was practiced much like that of the Hidatsa (Wilson 1917). Since the house distribution in the locality allowed sufficient garden space and fallow ground around each lodge, no need for frequent relocation existed as long as population density remained low. Given the adequate rainfall of the Neo-Atlantic climatic episode, which was the optimal period of forest development, vegetation cleared from garden space should have reestablished itself within a reasonably short time. With adequate rainfall, gardens would have been practical on the ridgelines. Locating in or near the oak-hickory forest zone on the tops of the ridgelines and hillslopes would further allow relatively easy access to major floral resources, the various nut crops. Since there is little evidence for large storage facilities in the lodges, Anderson and Zimmerman (n.d.:21) assumed that neither garden areas nor family size were large. The small house size also indicated a small number of residents in each house, probably a nuclear or small extended family. Anderson and Zimmerman therefore viewed the selection of house locations as favoring the ridgelines and hillslopes due to family structure, subsistence patterns, and environmental conditions.

With the onset of the drought-like Pacific climatic episode between A.D. 1150 and A.D. 1250, the settlement pattern began to vary. With the increased flow of dry westerly air, the practice of horticulture on the exposed ridgelines would have been less efficient than in earlier years. The oak-hickory forest zones would also have diminished in size, remaining only on the downslope protected areas. Eventually, horticulture would have ceased on the ridgelines and access to certain wild foodstuffs would have decreased markedly. If the severity of the drought were great enough to diminish food production or gathering below the carrying capacity, alternatives would be found to avert starvation by either moving from the locality or changing subsistence patterns. Consequently, ridgeline abandonment was predicted. More intensive occupation of protected valley floors and heavier reliance on gardening in well watered areas probably occurred. This would account for the clustering of houses in an effort to save valuable farm land. Also, residence groups were probably larger extended families.

Anderson and Zimmerman have provided a speculative model to account for the variable settlement pattern. They offer an extra-systemic cause for change that employs climatic fluctuation as an explanation. Their model was loosely structured and was consequently nonoperational for testing purposes, but it did provide some interesting insights into possible mechanisms for settlement change and locational behavior in the Glenwood locality. It is the Anderson-Zimmerman model that provides the basis for the model presented and tested here and some of their ideas will be developed more fully later.

5.   Modelling Goals

In solving a particular problem, the goals of the investigation largely determine the kind of model to be constructed. As research progresses, the goals may be altered, usually made more specific, but sometimes changed entirely or eliminated. The investigator must determine whether the goals have been met at the conclusion of research. To these ends, then, the goals of building a model to investigate Glenwood settlement patterns should be minimally stated before the investigation is very far along.

In general, these goals are:

1) To account for the variability previously noted in the Central Plains tradition settlement patterns of the Glenwood locality;
2) To understand to some degree the processes by which locational decisions might have been made by inhabitants of the locality;
3) To operationalize and test the implications of a number of assumptions about or reconstructions of Central Plains tradition culture for settlement patterns.

Specifically, an explanation of the settlement variability in systemic, dynamic terms is seen as desirable. It should, however, be phrased as realistically as possible so that the investigator can more readily understand its operation, including the impact of randomness on system behavior. Some means of testing the explanation is also desirable, preferably by the generation of simulated settlement patterns that can easily be compared to the known settlement distribution.

Investigation Procedures

A systemic approach to analysis of Glenwood settlement and subsistence was suggested in Anderson and Zimmerman (n.d.:15) as a means for the examination of factors influencing settlement patterns in the Glenwood locality. Their approach was a minimal effort to phrase the settlement analysis in terms of systems theoretical constructs. The analysis, though incomplete, was

41

beneficial in providing a general algorithm of how the settlement variability might have occurred. That algorithm is outlined below.

1) Populations culturally similar to those labeled Central Plains tradition began occupying the Glenwood locality between A.D. 800 and A.D. 900.
2) These peoples selected locations for their earthlodges on ridgelines, usually at some distance from their nearest neighbor.
3) Locations were probably in or near forested zones. In these zones wild foodstuffs were hunted and gathered. Slash and burn horticulture was minimally practiced in gardens near the lodge.
4) Nuclear family structure was the predominant residence grouping with matrilineal descent and proximal matrilocal residence.
5) This pattern remained stable until about A.D. 1200 when climatic change occurred.
6) Increasingly dry westerly winds brought decreased rainfall. The forested zones decreased in extent, especially on the ridges, causing a decrease in available resources.
7) Stress occurred on the subsistence base giving rise to intensification of horticulture.
8) With horticulture as the primary subsistence base, and the ridgelines too dry for such practices, subsistence activity focused on the stream floodplains and on low nearby hillslopes where the water sources were more consistent.
9) Lodge building locations shifted to these areas.
10) In an effort to save valuable garden lands, houses were built in small clusters and were larger in size to house extended families.

The major components of Anderson and Zimmerman's settlement "system" are present in the algorithm, but the precise nature of each is not clear nor are the linkages between them. As it stands, their assumptions and hypotheses are nonoperational and consequently nontestable. Further, their model is difficult to conceptualize in a realistic way because their system is constructed on too general a level and is not particularly dynamic in its approach.

Phrasing their model in a detailed, conceptually dynamic form was partially solved by formulating their system into procedures used for computer flow charting. The decision-making symbolism of flow charting made it possible to conceptualize the settlement patterns as a result of human locational decision making, a dynamic process. A simple open-ended flow chart was prepared (Zimmerman and Moore 1973) for location of a single lodge, a process that could be repeated many times for any number of lodges. The flow chart has been slightly modified and is presented in Figure 2.

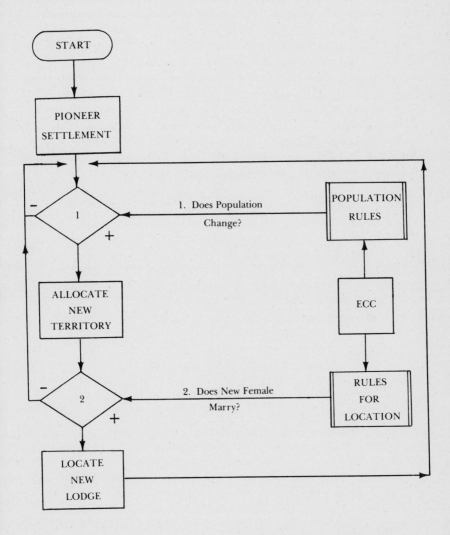

Fig. 2 *Simplified Flow Chart for Simulation of Settlement Subsistence Systems*

The basics of the flow chart are relatively simple. After initializing the system, the active core of the model, the population, is controlled via rules for birth, death, and mating. If the population changes, new territory to support that population is allocated near the lodge. If a new family is started, a new lodge location and territory are necessary. The locational decision is made from available locations via a set of rules. If the rules for a location are met, a new lodge is located. Both the population core and location rules are influenced by the environmental input by way of environmental carrying capacity (ECC). The ECC left open the possibility of environmental change discussed in Anderson and Zimmerman (n.d.). This flow chart moved the model toward being operational, but it remained too general; the flow chart is merely a device to aid in visualizing a model or process. To proceed beyond mere visualization requires more detailed systems analysis and model building. Mihram's (1972a) processes of systems analysis, synthesis, verification, and validation provide an organizing framework by which to build such a model.

6. Systems Analysis

Before a model can be constructed, it is necessary to understand what the salient components of the system are to be, what their interactions and relationships are, and what the system's behavior mechanisms are like. Analysis, therefore, includes definition and delineation of a system and its environment. In this chapter, the algorithm derived from Anderson and Zimmerman (n.d.) will be analyzed for the purpose of synthesis into an operational model.

The major components to be discussed are the system environment, population, social organization, subsistence, the system's behavioral mechanisms, and the locational rules. This analysis is built on the assumptions, inferences, and reconstructions of several cited authors. Those of this author as well as his theoretical positions will hopefully be clear.

The Glenwood Locality: System Environment

When Keyes (1951:340) defined the "Glenwood Focus of the Nebraska Aspect," he was referring to the remains of a distinctive cultural tradition represented by a large number of house sites located in the bluffs along the Missouri River in Fremont, Mills, Pottawattamie, Harrison, and Monona Counties in Iowa (Keyes 1949). Although sites were supposedly located in the other counties, Mills County had by far the greatest concentration of sites. When Anderson (1961) examined the Mills County materials excavated by Orr and established a local sequence, he also chose to more precisely define the manifestation by the Willey and Phillips (1958:18-19) definition of locality as ". . . a geographical space small enough to permit the working assumption of complete cultural homogeneity at any given time." Instead of discussing the area of bluffs outlined by Keyes, Anderson (1961:4) chose simply to define the Glenwood locality as an area encompassing a portion of bluffs and floodplain along the Missouri River in Mills County, Iowa. The area he defined was about nine miles by four miles. Figure 3 is Anderson's (1961:iv) map of the locality.

In dealing with cultural systems, a simple definition of geographic space occupied is insufficient. Recalling Mihram's (1972a:626) statements concerning delimiting systems, one must also be

45

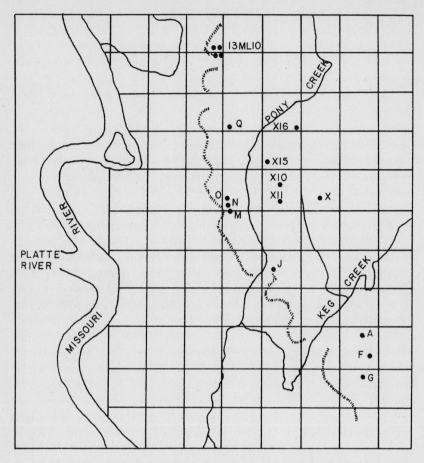

Fig. 3. *Anderson's 1961 Map of the Glenwood Locality*

concerned with a system's environment, i.e., "... those elements which, though they may from time to time affect system entities significantly, are never affected significantly by any of the elements (entities) intrinsic to the system." For most cultural systems, those elements are at least some segments of the natural environment that provide a behavioral setting in which the actors operate. In this particular model, which focuses primarily on subsistence and settlement systems, the key elements are the topography, climate, flora, and fauna of the Glenwood locality. Indeed, these elements do affect the system significantly, yet are little affected themselves by the system as it is modelled here. To understand the effect of the environment, a reconstructed overview of the Glenwood locality is presented. It must first be understood that little research has been undertaken to adequately reconstruct the natural environment of the Glenwood locality between A.D. 900 and A.D. 1300. Analyses of pollen samples and floral transects of the area are incomplete. Only one analysis of mammalian fauna from the sites has been finished (Johnson 1972), and Anderson and Zimmerman (n.d.) briefly reviewed the probable flora of the locality. Reconstructions were often made by inference from modern climatic, soil, floral, and faunal distribution. Extension of reconstructions into the past 1000 years is therefore tenuous, but as Butzer (1971:49) suggests, "the ultimate key to paleo-ecology is provided by modern distribution of similar features."

Climate

Butzer (1971:50) further acknowledges climate as the most important factor in the study of paleoecology. That he does so is not surprising; climate is responsible for major landscape features of the natural environment directly influencing weather, topography, soils, vegetational patterns, and animal distribution (Blumenstock and Thornthwaite 1941:99). As discussed in Trigger (1968), climate also plays a great part in locational decisions in cultural systems. Weather is largely responsible for architectural decisions made by the inhabitants of an area (Fitch and Branch 1960). Vegetational patterns and faunal distribution are integral to the planning of subsistence patterns. In this sense, climate is perhaps the most important element of a cultural system's natural environment. As noted, Anderson and Zimmerman (n.d.) use climatic change as a major causal factor for the shift in settlement in the Glenwood locality, an idea incorporated into the model presented here. Since climate is so important to the model, the important climatic features of the Glenwood locality, particularly the idea of climate change, bear discussion here.

The Glenwood locality occupies a unique climatic situation; it lies within subhumid prairie lands but near the humid eastern woodlands. In general, the subhumid area has a climate that is continental with relatively cold winters and warm summers (Trewartha 1941:168). Throughout the subhumid area there is considerable temperature variation from north to south throughout the year. In the Glenwood locality temperature extremes of -33 degrees and +115 degrees Fahrenheit were recorded during a 28 year period (USDA 1941:863). January temperatures drop to an average of 24 degrees F. and rise to an average of 77 degrees F. in July. The average number of frost-free days (27 April to 1 October) is 166. Bryson and Wendland (1967:295) place this locality between the -10 and -20 isobars in their determination of the annual precipitation minus potential evaporation rates. With an average of approximately 30 inches of precipitation per year, 77% of it between 1 April and 30 September, the area is slightly dry. Much of the summer precipitation falls in the form of sharp, convectional showers that are often accompanied by lightning and thunder. These showers are usually not long in duration but are relatively vigorous (Trewartha 1941:170). Winter precipitation is variable, often coming as snow, but snow cover is usually present on 30 to 40 days per year. Years of deficient precipitation are common in the subhumid lands, bringing reduced crop yields to modern farmers in the area. This yearly, local climatic fluctuation is common. Extended periods of fluctuation are uncommon, however, but appear to have occurred during the Nebraska phase occupation of the Glenwood locality.

A number of papers (Baerreis and Bryson 1965, 1967; Bryson 1966; Bryson and Wendland 1967; Bryson, Baerreis, and Wendland 1970) suggest that a climatic change around A.D. 800 was related to stronger movements of moist tropical air into the Great Plains. The extension of corn farming into Central Plains localities was supported by the generation of increased summer rains (Baerreis and Bryson 1965:215). This Neo-Atlantic episode, as it is named, coincides roughly with the Nebraska phase occupation in southwestern Iowa (Anderson and Zimmerman n.d.:9). A change in atmospheric conditions resulting in diminution of summer rains occurred late in the 12th century. Baerreis and Bryson (1967) based their studies of the Mill Creek peoples on cultural data and pollen, floral, and faunal samples from an area 100 miles to the north of the Glenwood locality. They noted that a probable increase in the westerly flow of dry air caused a decrease in rainfall and consequent availability of forest flora and fauna and prairie grasses. Hunting patterns shifted focus to the grassland species, bison, and corn horticulture was intensified. It has been suggested (Bryson et al. 1970) that the shift was relatively swift, probably occurring within a few generations.

This Pacific episode apparently lasted from A.D. 1160 to A.D. 1450, and ended the practice of corn farming among the Upper Republican peoples. By 1450, the climatic characteristics reverted to those of the earlier Neo-Atlantic episode. The change was only partial, and it is estimated that by A.D. 1550, with the onset of the Neo-Boreal episode, summers were cooler and the growing season was shortened in the upper Midwest. This episode lasted until 1880 (Baerreis and Bryson 1965:216-217). Although this proposed climatic sequence has come under attack (Butzer 1973), evidence provides support for it. Some are skeptical about a general drought severe enough to depopulate the Central Plains (Bryson et al. 1970), but it will be assumed to have had a definite impact on the Glenwood locality.

Geomorphology and Soils

The archaeological sites in the Glenwood locality are found on a series of rugged bluffs that form the boundary of the east side of the Missouri River floodplain. The bluffs lie within what Fenneman (1938) labeled the Dissected Till Plains, which have also been called Glacial Area, Dissected Loess-Covered Till Prairie, Missouri River Bluffs Zone, Bluffs Region, and Drift Hills (Gradwohl 1969:10). The major topographic feature of the area is, of course, the bluffs. The area was covered by both the Nebraskan and Kansan ice sheets, evidenced today by rolling hills composed of gray and tan tills containing cobbles and boulders. These tills are overlain by a mantle of windblown red Loveland and yellow Peorian loess (Gradwohl 1969:11). The loess deposits are in excess of 100 feet thick in many areas. The soils of the locality are of the Ida-Monona-Hamburg group of uniformly loess-derived loams, which are capable of supporting a wide variety of vegetation.

The Missouri River and its tributaries have sculptured this medium in the Glenwood locality into very steep to almost vertical cliffs, and in some areas of the locality, particularly in the northern Pony Creek drainage, the relief from the Missouri River floodplain to the top of the bluffs is nearly 400 feet. The Pony Creek drainage has the steepest hillslopes; in most areas the valley floor is seldom more than 200 feet wide except at the confluence of Pony Creek and feeder streams. Keg Creek appears to be a slightly more mature stream; the valley is wide, in many areas several hundred feet to nearly a mile. The bluffs near Keg Creek are considerably more rolling and much less rugged than those of Pony Creek. Both streams generally flow toward the southwest; both have permanent and intermittent feeder streams. Besides the two major stream valleys, the topography is also comprised of large, east-west oriented hollows formed by small streams that flow directly into the Missouri floodplain. These hollows are often a mile long with valley floors several hundred feet wide and precipitous valley walls. This ruggedly sculptured topography is the predominant picture of the locality: long, narrow, high ridges and intermediate secluded valleys.

Vegetational Distribution

The major topographic features of the Glenwood locality are the Missouri River, the first and second bottoms, tributary valleys, hillslopes, and uplands. Each feature is characterized by particular plant communities that provided basic vegetal food resources to the prehistoric inhabitants of the locality. These communities are referred to here as vegetational resource zones as defined by Zawacki and Hausfater (1969).

In their study of a transect of the lower Illinois River valley, Zawacki and Hausfater (1969:11) delineated ten plant associations ranging from habitats to communities. Each was characterized by a distinctive set of plants usable as food. These vegetal resource zones were narrow and generally paralleled the river and each other, giving them a linear character dictated by topography. Consequently, a kind of ecological stratification existed. As one moved from the stream bottom to the uplands, the zones seemed to be layered. A food gatherer could move for an extended distance within a single zone by paralleling the river or could move rapidly from one zone to another by moving perpendicular to the river. The effect would be relatively easy acquisition of large quantities of a few resources from one zone, or lesser quantities of many resources from several zones. These same features are roughly operative in the Glenwood locality with the zones paralleling both the Missouri River and the two major streams, Pony and Keg Creeks. The extreme dissection of the locality by small streams does disrupt the pattern somewhat.

These vegetal resource zones are described briefly to present an overview of the available plant resources from the locality as well as their general distribution over the landscape. The descriptions below, compiled by Anderson and Zimmerman (n.d.:4-8), are a synthesis of work by Weaver (1965, 1968) and Shimek (1911).

Lake, marsh, swamp zone. The floodplain, or first bottom, is marked by the presence of oxbow lakes, marshes, and swamps. Each of these maintains plant associations dependent on edaphic variables, most plants being riverine in character. The vegetation is composed of water lilies, pondweed, duck-meats, smartweed, and arrowhead. Swamps maintain perennials such as river bullrush, great bullrush, reed, bur reed, broadleaf cattail, arrowhead, and water plaintain. Marshes are characterized by tall species of grasslike sedges or such hydric grasses as reed canary grass and rice cutgrass together with smartweed, Canada anemone, water hemlock, iris, and various mints (Weaver 1965:42-46).

Floodplain prairie zone. Extensive areas of first and second bottomlands can be described as the floodplain prairie zone. First bottoms, where the soil is slightly drier and better aerated than swamp or marshland but too wet for big bluestem, are covered with prairie cordgrass. Prairie switchgrass, reed canary grass, and nodding wild rye also occur in this association (Weaver 1965:47-52). The terraces described as second bottomlands were covered by prairie as well, big bluestem being dominant (Weaver 1968:128).

Floodplain forest zone. The floodplain forest zone occupies areas of alluvial soils with better drainage than that occupied by the lakes, marshes, and swamps. Trees common to the floodplain are black walnut, red elm, white elm, ash, boxelder, and basswood. Shrubs associated with the floodplain are rough-leaf dogwood, smooth sumac, indigo bush, wild plum, wolfberry, American elder, coralberry, and wild gooseberry. Weaver (1968:127-128) also lists the following woody vines as common and abundant: frost grape, bittersweet, greenbrier, poison ivy, Virginia creeper, and virgin's bower.

The forest nearest the river is composed of sandbox willow (the first tree to occupy the banks of streams, lakeshores, and rivers) and both black and peach-leaf willow (Weaver 1965:37). The willows commonly form a border between the river and cottonwood forest, which develops on the moist sandy soils paralleling the river.

Tributary stream valley zone. Tributary stream valley systems such as Pony and Keg Creeks have, in addition to the primary valley, an extensive ravine system deeply eroded into the loess bluffs. Where the valley floodplain is developed there is an extension of the floodplain forest zone. The shelter provided by the ravines lends itself to habitat differentiation and disrupts the zone-paralleling feature noted earlier. Three forest community types that occur in the Missouri River valley (Weaver 1965:13-25) should have been present in the Glenwood locality where particular edaphic and climatic requirements are met. These community types, named for the dominant trees, are the red oak-linden, the black oak-shellbark hickory, and the bur oak-hickory communities. The black oak-shellbark hickory community is not found much farther north than Omaha and the red oak-linden community not much farther north than Sioux City.

In the Glenwood locality, the linden might be expected to dominate well-drained, moist, sheltered lower slopes intermingled with red oak. The red oak usually replaces linden about mid-slope where drainage is better; it is associated with shellbark hickory, which sometimes grows in nearly pure stands where the soil is slightly drier. Stands of bur oak usually appear on the drier uplands (Weaver 1968:135).

Hillslope zone. Hillslopes in the locality could be expected to exhibit two distinct vegetation zones. According to Weaver (1968:42), faces exposed to dry westerlies were probably covered by prairie grasses such as side-oats grama, which provided 10% to 60% of the plant cover on the steep xeric slopes. Needle grass is another species that could be expected to occur. This zone is much more common on the west-facing bluffs along the Iowa side of the Missouri valley. Shimek (1911) concluded that the combined effects of intense sunlight and hot dry westerlies common to the area prohibited the development of forests. Sheltered ravines and deep valleys within the bluffs, which were not subject to the drying conditions, were able to develop hillslope forest cover. The differentiation of forest community types discussed for the tributary stream valley zone pertains likewise to the areas where hillslope forest cover developed.

Uplands zone. Upland prairie, as defined by Weaver (1968:33), indicates soils of low water content. Upland grasses are little bluestem, needlegrass, prairie dropseed, side-oats grama, and junegrass. On the level prairie uplands, 50% to 75% may be little bluestem (Weaver 1968:38). Weaver (1968:84-93) reported that a total of 200 upland forbs were found but only 75 occurred with any regularity. Those common to the upland prairie include lead plant, prairie rod, dogwood, red root (New Jersey tea), Missouri goldenrod, prairie mugwort, stiff sunflower, prairie cats-foot, prairie clover (both white and purple), ground plum, Indian turnip, purple blazing stars, black-eyed Susan, false indigo, Pitcher's sage, blue-eyed grass, and yellow flax.

In order to suggest the degree of similarity between vegetal resources present in the Glenwood locality and the eastern woodlands, Anderson and Zimmerman (n.d.:8) compared those plants potentially used for food in the lower Illinois River valley (Zawacki and Hausfater 1969) with the plants found in the Missouri valley and bluffs adjacent to the Glenwood locality. Their assessment of presence or absence of particular species was based on species listed in Peterson's (1923) *Flora of Nebraska.* Since corroborative transects from the Glenwood locality have not been studied, comparisons remain untested.

There appears to be a general diminution of species as one proceeds northward along the Missouri River. Weaver (1968:129) noted that while broad-leaf deciduous forest heartland contains about 200 species, only 80 of which are found in southeastern Nebraska, that number is further reduced to 31 species in northeastern Nebraska. The three forest community types of the tributary stream valley zone are almost at the limit of their range (Weaver 1968:135). The 47 woody species listed by Zawacki and Hausfater (1969:16ff) are reduced to 22 in the Glenwood locality and the herbaceous plant species are reduced from 41 to 29. Considering the general reduction of species northward along the Missouri River, these reductions do not seem too great. Further, no attempt was made to include those plants with food potential that occur in the Glenwood locality but not in the lower Illinois River valley considered by Zawacki and Hausfater. In total numbers of species available, the difference between the more woodland, lower Illinois River valley and the Glenwood locality would not be great. It is further probable that the relative density of each species would be of far greater importance in determining food potential than simply numbers of different species. No such data exist for either area (Anderson and Zimmerman n.d.:9).

This cursory examination of the plant distribution in the Glenwood locality suggests that although the area is situated in a prairie biome, it maintains many of the characteristics of a deciduous forest biome, essentially structuring the ecotonal nature of the locality (Odum 1971). Perhaps the woodland character of the locality is not as impressive as the heartland of the eastern woodlands, but the importance of the woodland species for local subsistence should be emphasized. As Bell and Gilmore (1936:306) observed:

Thus, it is evident that while we are dealing with a region well within the Plains area, it is actually an extension of the Eastern Woodlands. Indians who had formerly lived to the south and east were not confronted by a significantly different geographical environment and hence, were not under pressure to adjust their culture. Any changes which came about would more likely be in the nature of acquisition of new traits in the response to the additional opportunities offered by the natural resources in the adjacent plains.

Faunal Distribution

Animal distributions are generally determined by the patterning of the flora on which they ultimately depend; many species are physionomically adapted to particular habitats (Butzer 1971:142). The range of most species is limited in some way to available plant food resources, thereby causing distinctive fauna for each plant habitat. The ecotonal nature of the Glenwood locality exhibits its own particular character; the animal community is composed of species from both the prairie and deciduous forest biomes as well as those species characteristic of the ecotone (Johnson 1972).

Few analyses of the Glenwood locality fauna have been done; most studies of the area are included as parts of regional syntheses (Jones 1964; Bowles 1972). The only detailed studies of the locality fauna from archaeological sites were done by Eshelman (n.d.) and Johnson (1972). These deal exclusively with mammalian remains from several of the earthlodges. Nonmammalian remains from recent excavations are currently being studied, but no results have been published. A total reconstruction of the locality fauna is impossible at this time, but Johnson's work will be summarized.

Johnson (1972) water screened all the excavated material from one earthlodge and sampled six others. He decided to analyze the mammalian remains only. His species list (Johnson 1972:54) of 27 identified mammals is presented in Table 2. Many of the species were limited to particular communities, but a number of them, mostly large mammals, were of multi-habitat association. In terms of the range of selection for hunting, all communities have some mammals.

Johnson (1972:53) also attempted to reconstruct the paleoecology of the locality in terms of the strength of association of the mammalian fauna with a particularly strong grassland association, suggesting a lack of trees around the site. He posits that the climate might have been warmer and drier during the occupation of the lodge than at present. This is indicated by the presence of the northern grasshopper mouse. House site 13ML126 was situated on a hillslope near the mouth of Pony Creek valley on the Missouri River floodplain. The mammalian fauna of three houses (13ML128, 13ML129, 13ML130) located in a cluster on a terrrace of Keg Creek exhibited more species common to the floodplain prairie community (e.g., eastern mole, rice rat, southern bog lemming), but both upland prairie and forest communities were represented. Three other hillslope houses (13ML131, 13ML132, 13ML135) had a similar assemblage. In all seven houses the rice rat appears; the Glenwood locality is at least 200 miles north of its modern range. No major climatic change was responsible for that variation (Johnson 1972:58). Johnson also notes that all other species recovered are or would be living in the area today were it not for human interference. Given the presence of the northern race of short tailed shrew from 13ML130, he suggests that the climate was not warmer

Table 2. *Mammalian Fauna from Glenwood Locality Earthlodges*
by Community Association

Floodplain (Moist) Prairie Community:
eastern mole
least shrew
plains pocket gopher
rice rat
southern bog lemming
meadow vole

Upland (Dry) Prairie:
thirteen-lined ground squirrel
Franklin's ground squirrel
plains pocket gopher
plains pocket mouse
deer mouse
northern grasshopper mouse
prairie vole

Lake-River Shoreline Community:
beaver
muskrat
raccoon
mink

Deciduous Forest Community:
eastern fox squirrel
eastern chipmunk

Forest Edge Community:
cottontail rabbit
eastern chipmunk

Multi-Habitat Association:
grey wolf
domestic dog
bobcat
deer
elk
bison

or moister than at present. With a radiocarbon date of A.D. 1235 for the lodge, he reasons that the house should have been occupied during the moist Neo-Atlantic episode but that would not have been possible given the climatic requirements of the shrew. That date is close to the beginning of the drier Pacific episode (Baerreis and Bryson 1965). However, it is now suggested that the Pacific began even earlier, perhaps at A.D. 1160 (Bryson et al. 1970:68). If so, the house would have been occupied well into the Pacific episode when the climate was warmer and drier, thus accounting for the presence of the short tailed shrew.

In short, the mammalian fauna alone do not allow adequate paleoclimatic reconstruction at this time. Baerreis and Bryson (1965:205) suggested that ecotone faunas are particularly suited for paleoclimatic studies because, ". . . with the species of two biomes already present, a climatic shift which brings a region more completely into the climate appropriate on one of these biomes should be readily reflected in changing proportions of species." Unfortunately, such changes in proportion were not obvious from Johnson's analysis, even though the presence of some species seems to indicate climatic variability. Demonstration may lie with further analysis that includes nonmammalian fauna.

The Probable Impact of Climatic Change

That a major climatic change occurred over the Central Plains or in the Glenwood locality has not been adequately demonstrated, but it is generally accepted by many Plains archaeologists (Lehmer 1954, 1971; Wedel 1959, 1961; Krause 1970). Anderson and Zimmerman (n.d.) used climatic change as a major premise of their model; climatic change will therefore be assumed for the purpose of this model. The impact of such change in the system environment of the Glenwood locality would be difficult to reconstruct precisely; the concurrent effect of change on the human inhabitants must also be tenuously reconstructed.

The effects of the changes on the vegetation within the Glenwood locality have not been determined, but certain assumptions can be made. Any climatic change that increases the flow of moist tropical air masses and decreases the flow of dry westerly air, which is projected to have occurred in the Neo-Atlantic (Baerreis and Bryson 1965), would favor the expansion of hillslope and upland forest zones and the decrease of the prairie grass cover in the same zones. If this assumption is correct, the Neo-Atlantic would have provided a more extensive woodland environment with its attendant woodland fauna, particularly deer and cottontail rabbit. For the aborigines this would mean abundant vegetal and animal resources, but it would also have expanded the potential for horticulture.

With the expansion of the prairie peninsula during the Pacific episode (Baerreis and Bryson 1965:216), reduction of forest cover in the Glenwood locality probably occurred. Prairie would most certainly have reappeared on the west-facing slopes and uplands, and the unprotected ridgelines would have lost the bur oak-hickory association, which would have retreated toward the better protected hillslopes and valley floors (Shimek 1911). The rugged topography in the locality might have provided an effective buffer from climatic fluctuation as Asch, Ford, and Asch (1972:24) suggest occurred in the lower Illinois River valley. With this buffer, the proportions of the various floral zones and their faunal communities would be affected, but none would disappear entirely unless the climatic change were extremely severe. Given the relative ease of accessibility to resource zones discussed earlier, fauna living in most zones could still be captured and many plants still gathered, but the availability of some species would decrease markedly while others increased. The concept of a buffer allowing preservation of species, together with the small sample size and the use of only mammalian fauna, probably accounts for Johnson's (1972) inability to demonstrate climatic change. The relative proportion of each species is the key, as mentioned earlier, and will ultimately give better information on the impact of the climatic change both on the distribution of species and the effect of that distribution on humans living in the area. Even with a topographic buffer, the proportions of floral and faunal forms would likely change with reduction in the number and density of woodland species. Such a reduction would probably reduce the hunting and gathering carrying capacity of the locality and would limit the practice of horticulture to areas with adeqate water supply. A shift of that intensity would necessitate a shift in subsistence emphasis and probably some major rescheduling of food procurement systems.

Modelling the System Environment

Natural environmental factors are themselves part of a dynamic system, but that system is related to the culture system only insofar as it provides the culture system with a medium for operation. When modelling the cultural system, attention should be focused mainly on the input of the medium to the cultural system and minimally on the consequential impact of the system on the medium. This, as a baseline for modelling, can limit the need for extensive analysis in an area with which the archaeologist usually has little expertise and, more often, little usable data. Even with proper knowledge of the relationships between environment and cultural system, no suggestion should be made that the environment is being used adequately or that its use is ultimately correct. In the model, the more complex the structure developed between environment and system, the greater the likelihood of error; it is therefore best to deal with the system environment in as simplistic a fashion as possible unless the modelling goals warrant more extensive usage (see Thomas 1972). These considerations were noted in the construction of the Glenwood settlement model.

For this model, the essential inputs of the system environment that required direct modelling links to the cultural system were climatic change, topography, and location of resource zones, all related directly to either environmental carrying capacity or selection of location. Topography and resource zones were relatively easy to deal with since topography was assumed to be stable for the duration of the model's operation and the resource zones were considered static in their locations until the climatic change. The climatic change presented some problems in that little was known about how the change occurred, its rapidity, or the precise nature of effects it would have on other environmental factors.

In dealing with the topography and resource zones, it was assumed that they are essentially the same today as they were during the Neo-Atlantic. Only with recent construction of highways, watersheds, and gravel quarries has there been any drastic shift in the topography of the locality. The assumption of stable resource zones is considerably more tenuous. If climatic conditions are generally the same now as during the Neo-Atlantic, one might be able to assume similar vegetal distribution today as in the past were it not for human interference. The extent of the recent human impact on the flora and fauna of the Glenwood locality is unknown. The rugged topography has prevented a great deal of cultivation except on bottomlands and wide areas on some ridgelines. This holds true especially for the Pony Creek drainage. Nearer Keg Creek the topography is considerably less rugged and therefore more land is under cultivation. The contemporary floral distribution in Keg Creek drainage is therefore less likely to be similar to the prehistoric distribution than is that of Pony Creek. Light foresting on the ridgelines near Pony Creek in recent years does, however, make actual distribution of forested areas questionable. There is no immediate solution to the problem that would allow firmer conclusions about the distribution of resources; perhaps pedalogical studies would offer corroborative evidence. No one knows the precise resource distribution in the Glenwood locality between A.D. 800 and A.D. 1300, so it is necessary to propose a hypothetical one based solely on modern distribution.

The modern resource and topographical data for the Glenwood locality were determined from USGS topographic maps; the Glenwood, Pacific Junction, Council Bluffs South, and Mineola quadrangles were used. A grid system was placed over the maps; the dimensions of the grid were 50 x 80 units. Each unit was based on the subdivision of a square mile into 100 units, making each unit approximately 6.4 acres in area and total coverage of the grid 40 square miles. In an area of rugged topography, 6.4 acres is a relatively large area from which to recover topographic data. Problems were inevitable. Topographic data were recorded to the nearest 50 feet based on the contour lines passing through the unit. In some areas of the locality elevation varied as much as 200 feet within a single unit. In those instances a rough average was taken. Averaging the topographic data and using large intervals of elevation could conceivably obscure the topography of the locality beyond utility; second generation maps based on such data might not be recognizable. To test this possibility, the grid system and the topographic data were provided to a number of plotting routines of the SURFACE II graphics package. Three maps were generated: one contour map and two three-dimensional projections with different elevations (Figs. 4-6). The contour map is surprisingly accurate (cf. Fig. 4); the projections clearly show Pony and Keg Creek valleys and the major hollows, and minimally show the terraces on the Missouri River floodplain. On the whole, the method of topographic data gathering was deemed adequate.

Five kinds of resource zones were established in the synthesis stage of modelling. Their designations reflect both topography and vegetal distribution. *River-floodplain* included both the floodplain prairie and floodplain forest communities discussed earlier under Vegetal Distribution. Since this zone in the Glenwood locality is vast, it was not considered particularly important to locational decisions and therefore was not allocated by the model. *Stream bottomland* provided access to water, the major consideration for location. This zone included the floodplain areas of the smaller streams, including Pony and Keg Creeks and their tributaries, as well as the floodplain areas of streams in the west-opening hollows. This category was difficult to identify since it included both grassland and forest areas that were essentially extensions of the river-floodplain forest. The major criterion used to separate the river and tributary stream forest areas was an arbitrary cutoff point of elevation; those areas under

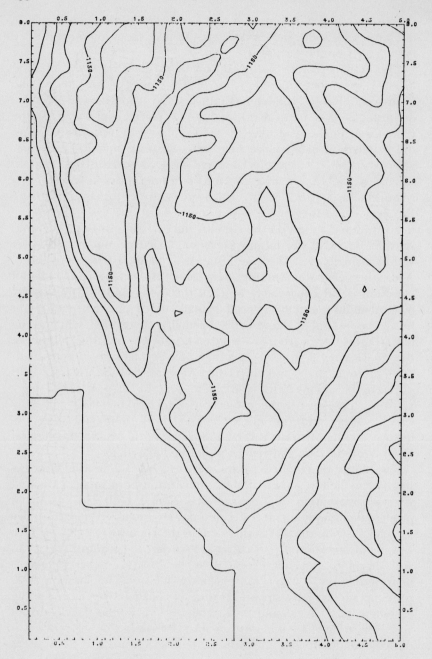

Fig. 4. *Computer Generated Contour Map of the Glenwood Locality*

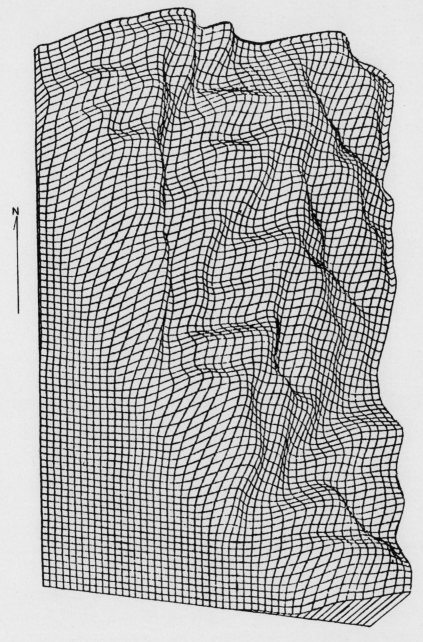

Fig. 5. *Three-Dimensional Projection of the Glenwood Locality: Elevation 60.0*

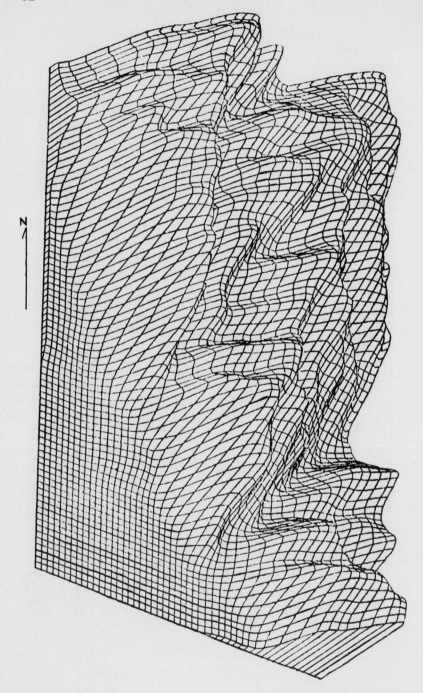

Fig. 6. *Three-Dimensional Projection of the Glenwood Locality: Elevation 45.0*

1000 feet were generally included as part of the river-floodplain resource zone. *Hillslope grassland* included both the hillslope and uplands vegetal zones. It was comprised of those areas where flora and fauna were grassland and grassland-oriented species. *Forest-grassland ecotone* included those units that were about half forest and half grasses. The fifth category, *oak-hickory forest*, included the three forest communities that comprised Weaver's (1965:13-25) tributary stream forest. This zone covered the ridgelines and valley hillslopes. Since its primary components were the abundant oak and hickory trees used for nut gathering, it was called oak-hickory forest for programming purposes to avoid confusion with river floodplain forest and to focus attention on its major resource. All resource zones were coded and recorded for each unit by observing the coloration of the topographic maps and checking the coloration against aerial photographs. In many instances the assignment was intuitive, but replicability was high. The areas that caused the most difficulty were those to be assigned as forest-grassland ecotone. These difficulties were seen as minimal since they did little to compound the existing problems of hypothesizing the distribution of flora and fauna of the period between A.D. 800 and A.D. 1300.

The climatic change, assumed to have occurred for the purposes of this model, caused some problems in analysis. Although some suggestions concerning the rapidity of the climatic change have been offered (Bryson et al. 1970:68), there is little information on how the change occurred and what its specific impact might have been on an area. On the basis of their radiocarbon date analysis, Bryson et al. (1970) suggest that the change was relatively rapid, occurring during a 50 to 100 year period, and that precipitation probably decreased gradually to about 50% of its former amount and then stabilized. The decrease per year for any particular locality was not indicated and would be difficult to accurately estimate. The precise impact on the distribution of flora is also difficult to know although some indication is given in Shimek's (1911) work. He suggested that the extent of forested areas on unprotected ridgelines and hillslopes of the bluffs was a function of the amount of dry westerly air flow over the area. The forested areas retreated to the more protected slopes and valley floors, and grassland covered formerly forested zones on ridgelines and west-facing slopes.

The concern here is not precisely how the change occurred, but assumptions about its general nature are necessary to operationalize the model. The impact on the distribution, proportion, and availability of various species is essential. Therefore, to account for the decrease in precipitation, it was assumed that the original amount of precipitation would be decreased by 5% every ten years for 50 years. Concomitantly, a decrease in the number of units of oak-hickory forest zone would occur in areas of higher elevation. Assuming that the first denudation occurs at the highest elevations, which are more exposed to the dry westerly winds, a decrease in the growth of trees above a certain elevation during a particular time span was postulated. During the first ten-year period, the forest would disappear in those areas above 1200 feet and be reduced in intervals of 25 feet over the next four ten-year periods until reaching 1100 feet. Those areas losing forest would become grass covered. In this way the effect of the buffering topography is implemented, but the impact of the climatic change is operationalized by the simple removal of a heavily relied upon resource zone. Ultimately, this sort of manipulation of the climatic change must be considered inadequate. However, given the available knowledge of the way the change occurred, implementation of the change for this model must remain relatively simplistic. The assumed structure of the climatic change is general and therefore flexible enough to be easily modified with better data.

Population

The construction of a model of a cultural system must realistically include demographic considerations; people are the locus of any cultural system. Archaeologists often seem to forget the people, emphasizing instead the artifacts they made. Use of systemic models at a supraartifact level has demanded some concern with demography. The publication of Wiess's (1973) "Demographic Models for Anthropology" in *Memoirs of the Society for American Archaeology* attests to that observation. The reasons for it are clear, as Wobst (1973:*vii*) says in the introduction to that volume:

> In explaining culture process, archaeologists have gradually traded in the simple cause and effect relationships, one-to-one analogies and straightforward inferences of the founding fathers for more and more complex networks of mutual causation. This trend has not only integrated archaeology more fully than ever before into anthropology and social science in general, but it has also greatly increased the area of mutual concern and potential cross-fertilization between archaeology and demography. One can safely predict that demography will assume a more important role in archaeology as we come to a better understanding of causation in the cultural realm.
>
> . . . Demography abounds in explanations of major evolutionary transformation: whether it is the rise of states or the origin of food production, demography provides one of the links in the chain of causation. . . .

Population as a causal factor in cultural change has gained considerable attention recently. Smith (1972) proposed the use of population as an explanation of change. Casteel (1972) provided two mathematical models for stable populations. Zubrow (1971b) was concerned with the relationship of population size and spatial distribution to environmental carrying capacity. Wobst (1974) dealt with the size and structure of Upper Paleolithic bands. Thus, the application of demographic data to archaeological problems seems fairly broad in scope and potential; its use is important in the model developed here.

Although Trigger (1968) does not mention demography as a determinant of settlement patterns, it must be considered as important as technology or climate. Perhaps population was implied in his use of social organization as a settlement determinant. Whatever the case, Zubrow (1971a) adequately demonstrated the role of demography in the development of settlement patterns. Population will therefore be treated as integral to the settlement system; it will in fact provide the stochastic core of the model developed here.

Two approaches to simulation of population growth have been used in archaeology to date. The first was a deterministic application of Neo-Malthusian exponential growth curves modified by environmental carrying capacity (Zubrow 1971a). The other was the Monte Carlo simulation employed by Wobst (1974). Deterministic models are particularly applicable when relatively precise population information is known for the culture in question or when the desired output of the model is simply a total population figure, as it was in Zubrow's case. The stochastic variety (stochastic and Monte Carlo are essentially synonymous) provides a more realistic approach to any detailed investigation of population change, growth, or composition.

Monte Carlo simulation is not as mathematically demanding as some of the deterministic mathematical equations (e.g., those presented in Casteel 1972). Hagerstrand (1967:372) suggests that Monte Carlo techniques imply ". . . that a society of 'robots' is created in which 'life' goes on according to certain probability rules given from the start." Wobst (1974:158) characterizes Monte Carlo simulation as ". . . an educational game consisting of a gaming table (area), pieces (people), rules (biological or cultural rules of behavior), and a series of different outcomes depending on the specifications of the components. Its educational purpose is either the isolation of the specification under which a given outcome was produced or the approximation of the outcome given a set of complex instructions."

The model to be used here has only four basic rules tied to the human life cycle. An individual is born, mates, produces offspring, and dies. The basic stochastic variables are when the individual is born, if and when the individual mates, how many offspring are produced, when they are born, what sex they are, and when the individual dies. These variables are controlled in the model by age-specific mortality rates (the probability of an individual dying within a given year), age-specific mating rates (the probability of an individual mating during a certain year), age-specific fertility rates (the probability of a mated female giving birth during a given year), and a sex ratio (the probability of an offspring being male or female).

These variabilities can be handled by the use of tables of cumulative probability, while the operation of the stochastic variables can be governed by uniformly distributed random numbers. Given the chance of birth, marriage, parturition, or death at a certain age, a random number between 0 and 1 is generated. If the number is larger than the probability, the event does not occur during the given interval; if smaller, the event occurs at the scheduled time.

It should be noted that the probability rates of the stochastic variables are closely linked to other segments of the cultural system. Mating in particular is linked to the kinship system. Mortality and fertility are related to such elements as subsistence patterns, disease, warfare, and environmental carrying capacity. For this model, the concern is essentially with the raw population data generated, i.e., the stochastic variables considered above. One set of life tables (Turner n.d.) will be used for the entire model (Tables 3-5). The cumulative probabilities will not fluctuate in response in relation to other system variables. In the real world the probabilities would be continually shifting; no attempt will be made here to achieve that level of reality.

The reasons for this simplistic use of demographic models are important to consider. Little is known about the composition of Central Plains tradition populations; from the Glenwood locality there is virtually no data. No skeletal material has been recovered. Attempting to alter life data in conjunction with changes in climate or kinship rules would be futile. In effect, all that can be hoped for is a set of estimated figures structured in a realistic way. This consideration must therefore remain a *caveat* in an analysis of results of this model; if the estimated figures are grossly different from reality, and the population system is at the core of the entire model, how accurate can the results of the model be?

Table 3. *Table of First Parturition (TPART)*

Age	Probability of First Parturition	Age	Probability of First Parturition
1	.000	22	.517
2	.000	23	.574
3	.000	24	.631
4	.000	25	.666
5	.000	26	.695
6	.000	27	.723
7	.000	28	.746
8	.000	29	.769
9	.000	30	.793
10	.000	31	.815
11	.000	32	.838
12	.000	33	.861
13	.000	34	.884
14	.057	35	.907
15	.115	36	.930
16	.172	37	.947
17	.229	38	.964
18	.287	39	.976
19	.344	40	.987
20	.402	41	.999
21	.459	42	1.000

Table 4. *Female (WMARG) and Male (MMARG) Table of Marriage*

Age	Probability of Marriage
1	.000
2	.000
3	.000
4	.000
5	.000
6	.000
7	.000
8	.000
9	.000
10	.000
11	.000
12	.000
13	.000
14	.000
15	.100
16	.200
17	.300
18	.400
19	.500
20	.600
21	.700
22	.800
23	.900
24	1.000

Table 5. *Female (WMORT) and Male (MMORT) Table of Mortality*

Age	Probability of Death	Age	Probability of Death
0	.00000	31	.06134
1	.00027	32	.06949
2	.00032	33	.07732
3	.00032	34	.08811
4	.00032	35	.09890
5	.00032	36	.11509
6	.00032	37	.13127
7	.00032	38	.14774
8	.00032	39	.16904
9	.00032	40	.20682
10	.00032	41	.23378
11	.00060	42	.26077
12	.00070	43	.28775
13	.00081	44	.31473
14	.00091	45	.34171
15	.00097	46	.36869
16	.00103	47	.39567
17	.00107	48	.42804
18	.00113	49	.46042
19	.00119	50	.49819
20	.00124	51	.53596
21	.00151	52	.57643
22	.00178	53	.61959
23	.00718	54	.66276
24	.01257	55	.70862
25	.01796	56	.75710
26	.02336	57	.80575
27	.02786	58	.85701
28	.03685	59	.90280
29	.04495	60	.95795
30	.05304	61	1.00000

Systems Analysis: Social Organization

The archaeologist often considers the role of social organization, i.e., kinship and residence, unimportant to locational decision making compared to the role of subsistence activities. Perhaps this is because the role of social organization is less directly tangible. That it is of importance seems to be implied by the term residence itself—people living somewhere. Trigger (1968:57) does in fact list kinship and residence as major determinants of settlement patterns. Its theoretical role in discussion of settlement patterns, however, far exceeds its actual role in efforts at analyses of settlement patterns.

The principal problem that has perplexed archaeologists is development of an adequate means to reconstruct this segment of cultural "software." The usual approaches are those of simple ethnographic analogy (e.g., Wood 1969), or reconstruction based on certain assumptions focused on a sexual division of labor (such as ceramic manufacture and traditional bases of artistic styles). The result has often been a statement of reconstruction using Murdockian (1949) terminology and seen as cultural prescriptions for behavior, such as matrilineal descent and matrilocal residence. This sort of reconstruction has been criticized recently by both ethnoarchaeologists (Stanislawski 1973) and sociocultural anthropologists (Heider 1967; Allen and Richardson 1971) as far too simplistic in concept. Since this issue of kinship and residence as prescriptive behavior is relevant to the way the system of social organization in the Glenwood locality is formulated, it will be discussed at length. For a more detailed discussion see Brockington (1976); many of the ideas presented below are based on his analyses.

The aftermath of the late 1940's and early 1950's debate over the nature of archaeology was a realization that archaeologists could do more than describe artifacts or order prehistoric units in time and space. Archaeologists could infer useful, albeit general, patterns of prehistoric social, religious, and political activities with the result that archaeology could ultimately contribute more to anthropology by extending studies of processes of change to areas other than technology. With refined methodological devices, especially multivariate statistics, inferences about social organization became relatively specific. The appearance of a number of case studies analyzing and describing post-marital residence (Longacre 1964, 1966, 1968; Deetz 1965; Hill 1966) and descent (Longacre 1964, 1966, 1968; Hill 1966) caused considerable stir. Brockington (1976:144) notes that "being new and perhaps somewhat shocking, the explicitness of these inferences has engendered some doubt and discussion of their propriety and usefulness." A recent paper by

Alien and Richardson (1971) summarizes the criticism leveled at archaeological inferences of social organization and attempts to demonstrate that the results of inferences of kinship and residence are "illusory or at best misleading" (Allen and Richardson 1971:4).

Allen and Richardson divide their discussion into separate critiques of inference for residence and descent. Concerning residence, Brockington characterizes their criticisms as following three courses of reason:

1) Archaeologists are using concepts of residence theory that are outmoded and current concepts are beyond the inferential grasp of archaeology.
2) There is too great a risk of error in such inferences.
3) The technical and methodological basis for drawing such inferences is unproven.

Justifiably, Allen and Richardson characterize most archaeologists as employing the residence concepts and categories developed by Murdock (1949), which imply that a particular society has and follows certain rules for the location of post-marital residence. The realization by social anthropologists that anomalies existed between "rules" and actual behavior, as exemplified in the Goodenough (1956) and Fischer (1958) discussions, caused the matter of residence to be reconsidered. The solutions offered in sociocultural anthropology focus on the determination of residence patterns by measuring or counting actual residence decisions that can be expressed in statistical terms instead of culturally prescribed rules (Brockington 1976:145). These patterns of residence can then be compared to the generally held "ideal" rules of residence often supplied by informants. This approach is similar to that suggested for ethnoarchaeology (Stanislawski 1973).

Brockington (1976:145) likens this discussion in social anthropology to questions raised concerning the usefulness and validity of the "mental template" concepts of archaeology. These concepts assume that an artifact maker has in his head a culturally prescribed "picture" of an acceptable artifact which he modifies idiosyncratically. Archaeologists can supposedly determine that template. Brockington argues that archaeologists have already been doing what Allen and Richardson claim they are not doing—using statistically determined residence templates while realizing that these rules are simply modal behaviors. On either side of the mode, other behaviors occur that in fact define the mode.

The two other categories of criticism are essentially

methodological. They are concerned with the nature of drawing inferences from archaeological data, especially those based on patterning in male and female manufactured artifacts. Brockington (1976:147) suggests that those inferences are merely hypotheses that remain to be adequately tested and should therefore not be overly criticized unless better, competing hypotheses can be offered.

Allen and Richardson's criticisms of inferences of descent from archaeological data again focus on the archaeologist's use of Murdock's terms. They suggest that there is not the one-to-one correspondence between post-marital residence and descent that archaeologists often seem to hypothesize. "They conclude that, because of this, and the fact that critical concepts such as corporateness are ambiguous and elusive, inference of aspects of descent is beyond the limits of the archaeological record" (Brockington 1976:149). They suggest that although all societies seem to be able to reckon descent, inferences about descent rules of prehistoric groups are misleading without specification of the purposes for which the rules apply (e.g., property and inheritance).

In their criticisms of both residence pattern and descent inferences, Allen and Richardson thus imply that archaeologists are unaware that prescribed descent and residence "rules" are ideals; such rules are often broken given circumstances that warrant aberrancy. Rules must be considered as "etic" only in the sense that they can be statistically defined as such, i.e., rules represent modal behaviors. Whether archaeologists really do consider these rules properly or whether the basis of their inferences is correct should not be at issue here. What is of importance is that these rules, whether statistically based or not, can and in fact must be considered as hypotheses to be tested. Further, these rules/hypotheses must be phrased understandably to be considered as modal behaviors; the purpose of their use by archaeologists must be made clear. Allen and Richardson's criticisms could have more effectively been aimed at such issues. Those issues will be of great concern when matters of residence and descent are considered in structuring the present model.

Central Plains Tradition Social Organization

Wood (1969:106-107) has reconstructed by analogy a probable social organization for Upper Republican and Nebraska phase peoples. His logic is related below and provides the basis for the analysis of the kinship and residence components of the settlement system used in this model.

Wood (1969:106) accepts Fox's (1967:83) premise that where

women are gardeners and men are hunters, as in the historic Plains village cultures, the ideal economic situation is for women to live in scattered settlements of matrilocal households where they can efficiently tend their gardens near their lodges. This assumption seems realistic in view of the dispersed nature of Central Plains tradition settlement patterns. Wood relies on Deetz's (1965:87-102) analysis of Arikara ceramics to bolster his analogy. Deetz argued that matrilocality and matrilineality contributed to a high level of attribute association in ceramics; matri-centered residence and descent provided distinctive ceramic clustering. The key is residence, and descent reinforces the pattern. Deetz suggests that major repetitive configurations in pottery could be produced by only four types of social structure: matrilocal-matrilineal, bilateral, patrilineal, and bilocal-matrilineal. Matrilocal-matrilineal should be most effective. His control sample of Lower Loup rim sherds from a protohistoric Pawnee site shows a high degree of attribute association. Deetz (1965:87) argued that:

> Protohistoric Pawnee ceramics, representing a culture known to have possessed consistent matrilocal residence, exhibit a high degree of attribute association, which in turn demonstrates the existence of rigorously channeled behavior patterns, probably transmitted matrilineally and reinforced by co-resident groups of female potters.

Wood (1969:106) also cites similar arguments by Longacre (1964) of closely related attributes between ceramic design and matrilocal residence in an east Arizona pueblo.

Besides the archaeological evidence, Wood also depends on ethnographic sources to confirm his ideas. He cites evidence by Eggan (1966:60-68) that regardless of descent, residence in Prairie-Plains tribes was generally matrilocal, the husband coming to live with his wife and her relatives in a multifamily lodge. Matrilocal extended families facilitated cultivation of crops by women and were consistent with matrilineal descent. Kinship was consistently lineal and descent patterns were vertical.

On the basis of these arguments by analogy and archaeological evidence Wood (1969:108) says:

> Theoretical considerations—plus liberal dependence on the historic derivatives of these people—lead to the possibility that one or more of the hamlets (plus related homesteads) of the Central Plains sub-area tradition comprised matrilineal, matrilocal groups composed of extended, polygynous (sororal) families. These residential units were organized into hunting bands led by natural leaders who held key

kinship positions between households exploiting common tillable land and gathering resources.

Wood's reconstruction, even though he admits it is untested, provides the basis for the analysis of the kinship/residence system to be used in the model built here.

The ceramic assemblage in the Glenwood locality appears to be relatively homogeneous. The typology developed by Ives (1955) and detailed by Anderson and Anderson (1960) indicates formal homogeneity. The seriations of Anderson (1961) and Zimmerman (1971) also indicate a temporal stability of ceramic morphology. No tests, however, have adequately demonstrated homogeneity. If these intuitions about the ceramics are accurate and if Wood's reconstruction is applicable, then the Glenwood locality Central Plains tradition peoples were probably matri-centered in kinship and residence patterns; matri-centricity will be assumed for this model. Two difficulties remained in formalizing this assumption for the model. First, what differences in structure and role of kinship and residence would be likely given the proposed shift from dispersed to nucleated settlement? Second, what is the impact of residence on population distribution and subsistence? That is, how can the kinship/residence systems interface with those systems?

Minor differences should occur if the population shifts from dispersed isolated lodges to small clusters of lodges due to environmental stress. Zubrow (1971b:137) suggests that carrying capacity disequilibrium causes aggregation to the extent that fewer larger extended family dwellings are constructed to maximize the use of available labor for exploitation instead of expending labor in construction. Further, available land is saved for exploitation as potential resource areas if less space is allocated to housing. Such circumstances could have prevailed in the Glenwood locality during the proposed climatic change.

With pioneer settlement in the Glenwood locality, adequate food resources should have been available to support several nuclear or small extended families (husband, wife, and daughter and family) by hunting, gathering, and minimal horticulture. Thus for this model, before climatic stress occurs, the major family unit will be nuclear or small extended. It should be noted that the Pawnee group on which Wood's reconstruction was based lived in relatively large compact villages (both archaeologically and ethnographically), making large extended matri-centered families possible. For the dispersed settlement groups, however, the pattern should vary since a large extended family unit would not be feasible. Further, from a cursory analysis of the Glenwood earthlodges, house size generally indicates small in-house populations. Isolated houses of the dispersed pattern are usually under 400 square feet in area, whereas the clustered lodges range from 400 to a reported 1600 square feet (Anderson 1961:1ff).

Presuming matrilocality as the major residence form dictates that marriageable males come from outside the locality. During pioneer settlement of the locality immigration would be vital due to the probable small local population, relatively few eligible males by age, and the likelihood of those males being too closely related to eligible females. Therefore, for this analysis, locality exogamy will be considered the prevailing marital mode. Given the nuclear family groupings, a strictly matrilocal pattern is not possible. Limited access to food resources would also indicate that newly married couples live outside the hunting/gathering/farming territory of the bride's parents so as not to overuse available resources. During the dispersed habitation period, this model will assume what is labeled here as proximal matrilocality, or neolocality, but with location as close as possible to the territory of the bride's parents. This pattern would preserve territorial exploitative norms for each family and allow a facsimile of matrilocal residence that would account for ceramic homogeneity.

During the period of climatic change, a shift from nuclear to larger extended family units should occur. The reasons for this shift, as based on Zubrow's (1971a) analysis, are discussed above. Locality exogamy is anticipated as the population should still be relatively small. The house clusters should form around matrilineally based kin units, probably clans, that resemble later Plains village groups. Since the available resources are decreased, aggregation should occur around elder sisters occupying parental territories in locations where exploitation would be necessitated. Exploitation would entail more intensive horticulture, which requires a larger labor pool, or more intensive hunting and gathering, which requires more man hours.

In sum, this unit analysis uses a matri-centric social organization based on Wood's reconstruction of Central Plains tradition social structure. Modifications and detail are provided to operationalize his concepts for the particular circumstances of the Glenwood locality and to interface the kinship/residence system to other model subsystems. The predominant features are outlined below.

Pre-climatic stress:
  1) Nuclear or small extended families are the predominant kinship grouping.

2) Hunting and gathering and horticultural territories are family owned.
3) Locality exogamy.
4) Matrilineal descent.
5) Proximal matrilocality.

During and post-climatic stress:
1) Larger extended families.
2) Exploitative territories are probably clan based for more efficient labor force utilization.
3) Locality exogamy.
4) Matrilineal descent.
5) Full matrilocality.

Regarding the criticisms of Allen and Richardson discussed earlier, for the purposes of this model the kinship and residence traits listed above are considered to be behavioral modes and are therefore hypotheses to be tested through operationalization of the model. In this sense, they act as cultural prescriptions and do not account for deviations or potential deviations from the mode. Consequently they are ultimately deemed unrealistic.

The Subsistence System
Little is known of subsistence patterns in the Glenwood locality. The only study completed concerns the use of mammalian fauna (Johnson n.d.) discussed earlier. Some plant remains, both domesticated and wild, have been identified (Cutler and Blake 1973:28). Any other reconstructions are therefore based on inference from other Central Plains tradition localities and ethnographic analogy. Although several reconstructions have been made, Wood (1969:103-104) provides a useful statement about Central Plains tradition subsistence; Anderson and Zimmerman (n.d.) dealt more specifically with the Glenwood locality and discussed the interface of subsistence and other natural/cultural systems. These two reconstructions provide the basis for the analysis presented below.

The northward movement of the Nebraska phase peoples was accomplished with increasing adaptation to local environments. The intrusion of these people with their horticulturally oriented subsistence base gradually dispersed the Woodland populations that had occupied the environments for perhaps a millenium. Nebraska phase populations first settled in small tributary stream valleys that emptied into the Missouri River floodplain, and eventually they occupied all major river systems and their perennial tributaries in the eastern Central Plains (Wood 1969:103).

There is ample evidence that Nebraska phase peoples grew the familiar American Indian triad of corn, beans, and squash using slash-and-burn techniques and the scapula hoe. The larger areas of tillable lowland soil available to Nebraska populations along the Missouri River suggests they practised more intensive horticulture than their Upper Republican counterparts. Dependency on hunting and gathering was considerable with the volume of wild plants providing abundant resources for Nebraska groups living near the Missouri mainstream. Since no hunting camps have been found (Wood 1969:104) to indicate extended annual hunts, it can be assumed that Nebraska peoples hunted only local game.

Wood's reconstruction translates well into the more specific subsistence pattern discussed by Anderson and Zimmerman (n.d.) for the Glenwood locality. They felt that the practice of hunting and gathering was as important to the Glenwood locality populations as horticulture, early in the occupation of the area. Both forest and prairie floral and faunal resources should have been available in abundance. Actual analyses of floral remains have been spotty. Cutler and Blake (1973:28) identified charred remains of many hickory and walnut shells from one house (13ML121). Based on Peterson's (1923) *Flora of Nebraska,* Anderson and Zimmerman (n.d.:15) compiled a list of 29 plant species that should have been available in the area. Few of those species have been represented in recovered archaeological remains. Johnson (1972) analyzed the mammalian remains from seven sites and listed species from the forest, prairie, and forest/prairie ecotone. His list (Table 2) suggests that Wood is correct; Nebraska populations usually hunted local fauna. Bison remains are relatively few and are found in no greater proportion than the predominant local large fauna (deer). Again, all fauna could have been taken in the immediate area. Preliminary analysis of avian remains indicates that turkey and waterfowl were utilized but in relatively small quantities.

During the pioneer period, horticultural activities in the locality were probably carried out as slash-and-burn gardening near the lodges. Equal or greater dependence on hunting and gathering, together with adequate Neo-Atlantic moisture and low population, would have allowed abundant garden space and fallow land near the lodge for each nuclear family unit. With more intensive horticultural activity after the onset of the Pacific, gardening would have been carried out in larger plots near the newly established hamlets on the valley floors and low on the hillslopes. In both pre- and post-climatic change horticulture, the variety of corn raised was probably ten-row. Beans were grown with corn as identified by Cutler and Blake (1973:23) from house sites 13ML119 and 13ML121. Squash, too, was probably grown, but no remains have yet been recovered from the locality.

The overall picture, then, is of a shifting balance between hunting/gathering and horticulture due to changes in the environment. The precise contribution of each technique at any one point in time would be difficult to determine given the present state of analysis of food remains from the lodges. General estimates of available edible biota for hunters and gatherers would be possible, but have not yet been made for the Glenwood locality. Estimates of the necessary maize acreage per person are based on studies of later Plains village horticulturalists (Will and Hyde 1917:108). Little useful, specific data is available then for the Glenwood locality. However, the variety of data suggests possible means for estimation of missing data and ways of articulating the estimates with population, kinship, and environmental systems.

For this model the contribution of wild food items and horticultural products is estimated as available food resources necessary for the yearly support of one individual. Kinds of resources are keyed to the environmental resource zones discussed earlier in this chapter. The grid system used to encode the resource zone imposed certain limitations on the subsistence model. The size of each grid unit was set at 6.4 acres, in most instances a generous amount of territory of each resource zone type for any individual. Given these estimates of resource requirements per individual, territories can be set for each family following Wood (1969: 103-104):

> Band boundaries are rarely drawn with any precision, for they are perhaps more often shaped by the availability of wild foods than by faunal resources. Gathering localities, whether 'owned' by individual households or communities, were undoubtedly all known—the stands of walnut, sunflowers, wild turnips and the like. Territories are often shaped by the type and number of gathering localities exploited by bands, with seasonal rounds dictated by the ripening of these plants.

In this model, each territory will be established by allocating a given number of units of each resource zone per household based on the number of individuals in the household. During the pioneer period, access to water would be the only reason to allocate stream bottomlands. Therefore, only one unit of bottomland will be assigned each lodge. After the climatic change, dependence on bottomlands for horticultural intensification will increase and allocation will shift to a "per person" basis. With the exclusion of stream bottomland, the initial allocation of resource zone units will be one unit per each adult in the lodge. Variations in number of units per individual can be implemented if desired.

In summary, subsistence practices are handled in an unsophisticated fashion necessitated by lack of realistic data. Resource zone units based on the grid system are allocated on a per person or per household basis; the number of these units per individual or household shifts with the climatic change. In a sense, this technique for establishing resource exploitative territories acts as a crude environmental carrying capacity—a function of available units of each resource zone type, requirements per individual, and the population of the locality.

Locational Rules

Since the focus of this model is ultimately the location of earthlodges, the rules by which the locational decisions were made by the inhabitants of the locality become primary for operation of the model. They are the integrative factors that link the subsystems of the model to each other and the environment. They must be the most precisely analyzed segment of the settlement system. Unfortunately, the information necessary to reconstruct locational behavioral rules is absent and must be inferred from the other subsystems and the known house distribution in relation to the environment. The information on which the inferences are made is likewise as weak. No statistical analyses of the known distribution (such as those suggested in Haggett 1965) have been done to provide clues. The rules, therefore, are intuitively based assumptions. They are further subject to the same *caveat* issued in the discussion of kinship and residence reconstruction: the rules, even though operationalized as prescriptive, must be considered as modal behaviors and not absolutes.

The theoretical position of the model builder is also of importance. Rules are necessarily stated as a list of priorities in decision making that would imply that the individual making the decision would have knowledge of the priorities and would be inflexible in rule application. Stated thus, the arguments about "economic man" being either optimizer or satisficer have relevance.

"Economic man" has the ability to always make the most beneficial decisions for himself. He would, in making these decisions, have some objective in mind such as the ideal location of his lodge so that he could most effectively meet resource requirements or social obligations. This behavior has been viewed as either optimizing or satisficing; the former seems to have little basis in reality. The optimizing economic man would have to have perfect knowledge of the situation with all its options as well as perfect ability to exercise those options in order to continually make the best decision. The satisficer, on the other hand, does not always have to make the best decisions; he has neither perfect knowledge nor perfect ability to use that knowledge. He has a goal in mind that will minimally meet his needs. He uses a limited set of rules to make a decision. If two or more choices are left after he has eliminated those that will not meet his goals or satisfy his needs, his choice between the alternatives will essentially be random, perhaps based on some quickly invented ad hoc rule. Following Pred (1967), as more and more decisions of the same type are made, knowledge and ability are increased and the decisions become progressively more optimal.

The satisficer behavior is the approach to locational rules conceptualized here. The rules developed here were meant to be minimal and directly linked to elements of several subsystems; the possibilities for rule formulation were limitless. The major rules used here are focused primarily on territorial allocation and post-marital residence.

The primary locational rules are economically oriented. A lodge must be located in an area where there is adequate resource potential to support a nuclear family unit. This rule is directly linked with the subsistence system that uses a hunting/gathering/ horticulture territory composed of units of each resource zone per family. Within that territory are a number of potential lodge locations. Since it was established that the subsistence base was an even mixture of hunting/gathering and horticulture and that adequate rainfall would have been present to grow crops on the ridgelines, the ideal location would be near the primary hunting and gathering zone, the oak-hickory forest. The forest zones with relatively dense cover impede the cultivation of domesticates and pose certain problems since trees or bushes would have to be cleared. The ideal situation would therefore be in a resource zone of the ecotone variety. Since at least two of these units would be necessary for a nuclear family, another choice exists. The decision depends on the topography of the area with location being chosen in the ecotone unit with the highest average elevation. There is the possibility that there could be several choices if the units are of equal elevation; if so, the selection is random.

These rules function once a territory is selected, but it can safely be assumed that in an area of 40 square miles, several territories of adequate size and composition would be available to support a nuclear family. The selection of an area for a new territory and house location becomes important when an eligible female marries and a new household is established. The location of the new territory is managed by the proximal matrilocality residence mode. A search is made for the available adequate territory nearest the bride's parents. Within that territory, the precise lodge location becomes a function of subsistence and topographic rules. The last daughter of a family to marry does not establish a new lodge, but instead takes over the parents' lodge and territory.

As the transition to drier climate occurs, the territorial requirements will not be as easily met, putting stress on existing lodges. Newly married couples will be unable to find adequate territory to support their lodge. A true matrilocal residence pattern would emerge with environmental pressures eventuating a shift in subsistence strategies toward an intensification of horticulture. Bottomlands, with their fertile soils and ready water supply, then become the optimal resource zones for cultivation. The locational rules that result are descent based. A rule is phrased such that territories "collapse into a matriline;" that is, aggregation would occur around matrilineal kin. If the parents survive, they and their daughters and families would move to the parents' area of bottomland to build one extended family lodge. If the parents are not alive, the aggregation occurs around the eldest surviving daughter and her territory. Given relatively localized, large areas of stream bottomland near the confluence of streams or in hollows, it is likely that several extended families would locate in the same general area. Given the pretransitional rule of proximal matrilocality, the assumption is made that those in the same area would be matrilineal kinsmen. The end result would be small clusters of lodges inhabited by matriclans and built in limited space to save valuable crop land. Each lodge would house an extended family based on surviving members of the formerly dispersed nuclear family units.

It should be recognized that the rules are essentially deterministic in their structure except in the instances where equal alternatives to location exist and no rules for decision making have been formulated. The rules are, however, a series of mutually interacting imperatives; the strength of their function is set by their interaction. Existing rules "play off" each other until a satisfactory, not always optimal, location is found for each lodge. Randomness is involved in some segments of locational selection—first in terms of the available set of location/territories when a new lodge is to be established and

82

second, when equal alternatives present themselves. The possibilities for expansion of these rules are infinite. Perhaps one could eventually eliminate all random factors or even phrase locational rules in terms of optimization; neither is viewed as adequately realistic for the purposes of this model.

Summary

Systems analysis provides the base on which a model is built; it is a framework to which continual reference is made as system synthesis occurs. In the systems analysis stage, weaknesses of various model segments exist that often do not become apparent until programming of the model is actually under way. Certain segments had a much larger data or assumptive base (e.g., environment and population) on which to build components and linkages. However, the length of the discussion of each is not a good indicator of analytical thoroughness. The locational rules pose the fewest problems for synthesis and the environment the most. Many of the difficulties with the system structure only become apparent during the verification stage of model building. Systems analysis becomes a continually reiterative process as diagrammed in Figure 1. Ultimate boundaries must of course be realized lest one become trapped in the complexity dilemma. The following chapter, System Synthesis, will clarify some of the items discussed in this chapter and will suggest where boundaries in realism of model construction were set.

7.   System Synthesis

Since many of the synthesis operations are conceptualized in the systems analysis stage, the major tasks of the system synthesis stage are the selection of the variety of model to be used and construction of the prototype of that model. By the time the problem has been conceived and the system analyzed, the model builder generally has an excellent idea of the type of model he wishes to employ. Such is the case here.

Since the major concern here is with processes, i.e., transformations from one state to another, a dynamic variety of model would probably best allow the operation of the process to be followed and more easily structured. The use of material models would be feasible if only the tangible aspects (e.g., lodges, locations) of the system and system environment were being considered. The concern here with subsystems that are ideological (e.g., social organization) or that involve a large number of variables, makes adequate material models difficult to conceive. Symbolic models offer the best alternative since one can describe a kinship system or a set of residence rules. Further, although a series of mathematical symbolic models might be formulated to deal with the processes modelled for the Glenwood locality, the model builder often possesses neither the knowledge nor ability to do so, as is the case here. Reliance must be on natural language constructions that can be relatively easy to comprehend and therefore make the system more tractable. The model, although deterministic in part (the way climatic change occurs for instance), has elements that are not deterministic. The population subsystem, which is the major segment of the system that has a series of random components, makes stochasticity imperative to retain the desired realistic character of the model.

Thus far a model that is dynamic, stochastic, and symbolic in nature is seen as desirable. The complexity of such a model and the quest for realism suggest that a simular model would be the most efficacious. As Wobst (1974:158) simply puts it, "a complex situation cannot be carried out without the use of the computer."

If a computer simulation is to be the goal, a programming language must be selected that best suits the needs of the model

builder and is easily accessible to him, both in terms of the computer
system on which he will be working and in terms of cost. In the
synthesis of this model the simulation language SIMSCRIPT was
chosen. SIMSCRIPT is an event oriented algebraic language of
FORTRAN-like words, phrases, and symbols. It is a generalized,
almost natural, language and therefore applicable to a wide range of
problems, making it a useful tool for organizing, analyzing, and
modelling both the structure and behavior of complex systems
(Honeywell Information Systems, Inc. 1972:1-1).

SIMSCRIPT Concepts

In the SIMSCRIPT language the elements of the system being
modelled and simulated are described by their attributes. The
behavior of the system is simulated both by assigning the elements
under consideration to membership in predefined sets and by
changing the values of the attributes associated with the various
elements. The status of the simulated system is described at any
certain simulation time in terms of entities, their attributes, and sets,
which are similar to the state variables discussed in Chapter 2. This
status is modified at various points in simulated time by the
occurrence of events. Entities, attributes, and sets provide the data.
Changes in system status are accomplished by the execution of event
routines that act on the data.

Entities are those objects, such as people or lodges, that are
considered in the simulation model and are defined as either
permanent or temporary. *Permanent entities* are those that are stable
enough to be included in the simulation on a permanent basis, i.e.,
throughout the duration of the run. The number of permanent
entities must be constant for each run, but can vary from run to run.
A *temporary entity* is transitory; its entry into, residence within, and
departure from the sytem are controlled by the programmer. The
number of temporary entities within the system can vary through
simulated time. Considerable flexibility can be allowed in the
definition of entities; definition depends on the nature and cost of
the simulation. Entities will not usually be of one type or the other,
but will be mixed. Temporary entities are more difficult to keep
track of than permanent entities, but require less storage space and
therefore less cost.

Attributes are those characteristics that describe entities. They are
variables whose values may be set, changed, or used in computations
and decision making during the run. *Permanent attributes* describe
permanent entities and *temporary attributes* describe temporary
entities. The former require permanent storage, while the latter

require storage allocated from a storage "pool" when the entity is created. When the entity is destroyed it is returned to the "pool."

A *set* is a collection of entities that are related to each other in some way. The set may be owned by or associated with a single entity or with a pair of permanent entities or by the system itself. For any particular set, the member entities must be either exclusively permanent or exclusively temporary. For any specific entity, whether permanent or temporary, membership in one kind of set does not preclude membership in other kinds of sets concurrently or at different points in simulated time. The exception is that the entity not be a member of more than one set of the same kind at the same time. Members of a set are organized according to the order they enter or leave the set under processing defined as normal by the programmer. Such organization is a property of the set itself. The organizational schemes are: first-in-first-out, in which the first entity to enter the set is the first to leave it; last-in-first-out, in which the last entity to enter the set is the first to leave it; and ranked, in which some attribute of the entity is used to determine the priority of its removal from the set.

Changes that occur in the real system are simulated in SIMSCRIPT by *events* that may be exogenous or endogenous. *Exogenous events* are changes in the system caused by factors external to the sytem, i.e., the system environment. *Endogenous events* are changes having causes internal to the system itself. When either type of event occurs, various changes take place in the status of the simulated system. These changes are described by event routines or programs that are automatically executed at a given point in time as a result of prior scheduling of the event. Each kind of event has its own event routine that specifically describes what changes are to take place by altering attribute values and by changing set memberships and ownerships. There are no restrictions on the number of different events; any event may recur repeatedly throughout the program or once at a desired point in simulated time. A specific endogenous event is scheduled by a statement in some prior event routine, whereas exogenous events are scheduled to occur during execution by entries in an Exogenous Event File supplied by the user. Such entries indicate the kinds of events and the simulated times at which they are to occur.

A special type of temporary entity called an *event notice entity* is associated with the endogenous events. Its primary function is to hold the time and priority for the occurrence of the endogenous event. It may also have attributes that are used to transmit information to an event routine.

A *timing routine* monitors and advances simulated time according to the occurrence of exogenous and endogenous events. To generate the timing routine the compiler requires an events list. A list of endogenous, scheduled events (a ranked set of event notice entities) is inspected by the timing routine following the occurrence of each event. The endogenous event notice with the earliest time is selected and its time compared with the next exogenous event; it then selects the earliest. Simulated time is advanced and the appropriate event routine is called into operation. Upon completion of the activities in each event routine, control is returned to the timing routine. Simulated time is not necessarily advanced in even increments.

The SIMSCRIPT language consists of words, phrases, and symbols that specify the operations to be performed in the model. Eight different types of statements are formed from these language components to describe each step in the simulation. Entity statements specify the operations to be performed on entities. Control statements govern the iterations of statement executions. Arithmetic statements specify computations to be performed. Decision statements alter the normal sequential execution of statements. Selection statements select and identify variables within specified criteria. Input/output statements provide the necessary input/output routines and formats. Routine and subroutine statements define and call subprograms and event routines. Specification statements provide information about variables used in the program.

The SIMSCRIPT language is similar in structure to FORTRAN, but has capabilities beyond algebraic functions. It is designed especially for simulations of the variety developed here. The language is not particularly complicated because it is much like natural language. It does present some difficulties in structure when building a complex program such as the one presented below. The system must be well analyzed before the programming actually begins. Even with the most logically structured analysis, it is likely that adjustments will need to be made, especially in attribute specification of entities and precision of event routines. The archaeologist may not realize the various problems until programming begins, but flexibility is a major beneficial attribute of SIMSCRIPT that must always be kept in mind. Such cautions are the result of difficulties encountered in the original efforts at building the prototype of the model of Glenwood locality settlement and later efforts at debugging the program during the verification stage of analysis. The prototype of the model is discussed below; a program list of the prototype is presented with minimal documentation in the Appendix. Later versions of the program are substantially the same with mostly minor changes in some events and initialization.

Glenwood I

The structure of the Glenwood I program follows the tenets outlined above. It is based on a very general conceptual prototype, Simulation for Anthropological Modelling (SAM), prepared by Zimmerman and Moore (n.d.). The SIMSCRIPT program consists of a series of exogenous events for starting the program, changing the climate, and terminating the program as well as several endogenous events for in-system manipulations such as birth, marriage, death, and seasonal change. Linking the events is a series of subprograms consisting of SIMSCRIPT statements. Both the events and subprograms operate on and manipulate sets of data that are the entities. Each major event, subprogram, and entity will be described here. The description includes in parentheses the pertinent line numbers from the program list in the Appendix.

Entities. In the systems analysis, population was made the stochastic core of the model with descent and residence rules affecting the structure of the population. Consequently a temporary entity WOMAN (80) was defined. This entity owns a set of other WOMAN-related sets representing attributes of a female and her daughters. Each woman is the daughter of another woman referred to by an attribute of the WOMAN node, MOTHR, which is also contained in a permanent entity MATRH (220). MATRH is used to contain information about a matriline after a woman dies. In this way, property rights and formation of extended family units after the climatic change can be expedited. WOMAN also contains attributes about the set of daughters of each woman, FDAUG and LDAUG, as well as a set of daughters of which this woman is a member (SDAUG). The MATRH and WOMAN entities are conceptually difficult, but are the major entities of the system. Figure 7 is a schematic of the WOMAN node concept and demonstrates its role in record keeping.

The WOMAN entity also has information attributes linking each node to other entities. LODGE points to the lodge entity in which the woman resides. SRESI points to the set of residents with whom the woman resides and FCHIL/LCHIL points to her set of children. Other attributes contain information about the woman's birth and death dates as well as the same information for her spouse.

88

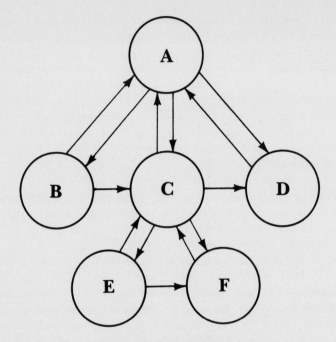

Fig. 7. *The Woman Node Concept*
Each circle represents a WOMAN node. A is the mother of B, C, and D
and the grandmother of E and F.
C has sisters B and D and married female children E and F.

Each WOMAN can have a pointer to the mother (⋏) as in B, C, D, E, and
F; is a member of the set of married sisters (↦) as for B, C, D, E, and F; and
can own a set of married daughters (⋎) as A and C do.

The LODGE (245) entity contains information about the
earthlodges that are constructed and inhabited. SHAUS is a pointer
to the entire set of lodges existing in the sytem. FRESI points to the
set of residents who inhabit the lodge. The other attributes are
descriptive, including the date of construction (DCONS), size (SIZE),
and location of the lodge on an X-Y coordinate system (LOCX,
LOCY). Also contained in LODGE is information about the amount
of territory controlled by the lodge in terms of the number of units
of each allocated resource zone type (NTYP1-NTYP4). During and
after the climatic change a logical variable (FARM), i.e., true or false,
notes whether or not the lodge inhabitants have intensified
horticulture.

A temporary entity CHILD (370) belongs to a WOMAN entity to
hold information about each of her children. SEX indicates the sex
of the child. BDATE, MARDT, and DDATE indicate the birth,

marriage, and death dates respectively. SCHIL points to the next child in a WOMAN's set of children and is simply a marker.

Events. The data contained in the entities are altered or manipulated by the events that occur during the simulated time span of the system. Since this simulation is to run as long as 400 years, an unusually long duration for most simulations, the variable TIME is used to represent years instead of days or hours. Thus, for this simulation, a day consists of twelve hours with each hour representing a month.

There are three exogenous events: START (1080), TRNS1 (1520), and STOP (1615). START begins the program at the selected starting year and sets up the system. TRANS1 is the major climatic change scheduled to occur later in the program. STOP completes the activity of the program.

There are five endogenous events that occur often within the system. SEASN (1630) occurs periodically to conduct system maintenance, checking the status of needed or added territory, births, deaths, and locational changes of lodges and their inhabitants. MARY (1920) is an event that occurs when a female child marries. DEATH (2615) occurs when a WOMAN or her husband dies, and BIRTH (2410) occurs when a CHILD is to be born. SNAP (2990) occurs regularly to print out information about the system. These events are used in conjunction with a number of subprograms. The events and subprograms are outlined below in the sequence of their operation.

Output. The most important information produced by the program is the simulated locations of the earthlodges and their dates of occupancy. This information is available from the line printer in two complementary forms: a table showing the location and all pertinent data for each lodge, and a map showing lodge territories. Additional data are also printed to show population levels and composition. The locational information allows ready comparison of the simulated settlement pattern to the real pattern for validation purposes; the other information assists in verification of the model by providing system status reports.

Operation of Glenwood I. The intent in this section is to provide more information about how Glenwood I operates and the nature of the events and subprograms in particular. The reader should again refer to the program list in the Appendix. In the text below, program list line numbers are again provided.

After the entities, their attributes, and events have been defined (80-1075), the program commences with exogenous event START. The principal function of START is to initialize the system. A map of the Glenwood locality is constructed in the form of a 50 by 80 array with information on the elevation and resource zone type as described in Chapter 6. START then creates the initial WOMAN nodes and LODGEs. Values such as birth dates, X-Y coordinates for the lodges, and dates of construction that were previously set by the programmer are now incorporated as attributes of the entities. Death dates are scheduled for all individuals and marriage dates for those unmarried children. Births are scheduled for each original woman according to the established probabilities for age and number of children. Each CHILD entity is established and marriage dates are scheduled. For each LODGE, based on the number of occupants, territory is claimed from the necessary resource zones by calling subprograms Claim Territory (CLRTP), Territory Type (TRTYP), and Territory Add (TRADD). START also schedules SNAP to print out data and SEASN to do system maintenance. START is perhaps the most crucial of the exogenous events in that it sets the initial status of the system and schedules all future major events (TRNS1).

The scheduling of events also occurs from other events. SEASN (1630) is the main time-controlling endogenous event that schedules other events. At equal time intervals, in this case a simulated three months, all WOMAN nodes are accessed through their LODGE and maintenance is done. For each lodge the current territorial requirements are monitored by calling CLRTP and TRTYP; if territory is needed, TRADD is called and the necessary units are added. SEASN also checks to see what births, marriages, and deaths have been scheduled; if during that time interval such events are scheduled, SEASN carries out the activity. With maintenance done, SEASN schedules the next SEASN. The subroutine TRACE prints out all occurrences of SEASN and lists the subsidiary events with their exact time of completion.

The other endogenous events, with the exception of SNAP, occur less regularly and as a function of the population core of the model with births, deaths, and marriages. Each of these endogenous events is described below but not necessarily in the order of their occurrence.

Endogenous event MARY (1920) schedules the mating of each female child according to an age-graded table of probabilities for marriage, WMARG. Each female marries a male from outside the locality. As she marries, a new WOMAN entity is created and her husband is assigned a birth and death date. She is then checked, from an age-graded table of first parturition (TPART), for the probability of having her first child. If she is to have a child, endogenous event BIRTH is scheduled. If this new WOMAN is the last female child of a family to mate, she continues to live with her parents in their lodge to ultimately take over their territory as in ultimogeniture inheritance rules. If she is not the last daughter, she is removed as a child from her mother's WOMAN node and sets up a new LODGE if enough territory is available. If territory available to meet the needs of the new family is insufficient, the new bride leaves the locality.

The major functions of endogenous event BIRTH (2410) are to set up new CHILD entities within each WOMAN node and to schedule the next birth. The CHILD entity is a compilation of attributes. The child's sex is determined by random number generation, 1 being female and 0 being male on the basis of an idealized 1:1 sex ratio. Birth date equals the current system time. The child's marriage and death dates are also scheduled by random number generation procedures in conjunction with the age-grade tables of probability. The next birth is scheduled by determining the number of children a woman has had, incrementing her age by two years (functioning in effect as a post-partum sex taboo), and checking her age and a random number against the table of first parturition, which has been altered by a factor of .9 to decrease the probability of another birth immediately after the prior birth. If she is scheduled to die in the two year interval following the birth of a child, no new births are scheduled for her.

The major function of endogenous event DEATH (2615) is to carry out the deaths scheduled in BIRTH or MARY for a woman, her mate, and any children. It further has a set of functions related to the descent system and inheritance. If both parents have died and unmarried children survive, those children are removed from the WOMAN entity of their mother and are transferred to that of a kinswoman. The DEATH routine searches the MATRH entity for the eldest married female child of the dead woman and her husband. If no married child is found, a search is made for the eldest living married female sibling of the dead woman and so on until a suitable home is found. If a suitable home is found, the unmarried children are transferred; if not, the children are removed from the system. In any case, if there is no married daughter living in her parent's territory and lodge, the lodge is abandoned and all its territory is released to the system for reallocation to newly forming lodges or those needing additional territory. If a married daughter is living with her parents, the territory is not released to the system, but a new lodge is constructed on the next highest territorial unit of the ecotone type. Endogenous event SNAP has the simplistic, but important, function of displaying a map of territorial claims within the Glenwood locality every simulated five years. The map consists of the 4000 grid units, based on the original 50 by 80 grid for recording topographic and environmental information. Each unit that has been claimed as territory by a particular lodge is marked by a symbol for that lodge. Figure 8 is an example of the territory initially claimed by the lodges during the time interval between A.D. 905 and A.D. 910. Each symbol indicates the territorial units for a particular lodge. SNAP allows a simple graphic display of one status variable, territory.

Subprograms. The ten subprograms of Glenwood I are the "workhorses" of the system; they carry out the basic manipulations of data and the major output operations. LGLOC, CHECK, MOVE, RELE, and CHANGE are all involved in the location of a lodge for the newly married couples or in the relocation of a lodge given adequate situations for locational change. CLRTP, TRTYP, and TRADD are directly involved in the acquisition of a lodge's territory. PWOMN prints out information about each WOMAN and LODGE entity and HSIZ allows for changes in family size that necessitate larger houses.

The procedures for establishing the first lodge locations in the locality are accomplished by exogenous event START and the initialization set by the programmer. If new lodge locations are necessitated as a bride marries, if the lodge inhabitants die, or if a new location is needed because suitable territory cannot be found at a current location, a series of subprograms is called by the system: LGLOC, CHECK, MOVE, RELE, and CHANGE. LGLOC takes the current X-Y coordinates of a lodge (either a bride's parents' or a WOMAN's own lodge) and seeks acceptable locations within a half mile radius of the established lodge. This is done by calling subprogram CHECK, which computes an Acceptability Ratio based on the number of units of each resource zone type within a 2.5 mile radius. If adequate territory is not available, either because it does not exist or is already claimed by another lodge, a new check is made until an acceptable position is found. When located, the center of the territory is noted and from that point a search is made for the ecotonal unit with the highest elevation. The lodge is located within that unit. CHANGE is called from endogenous event DEATH when a female resident inherits her parents' territory. She establishes a

93

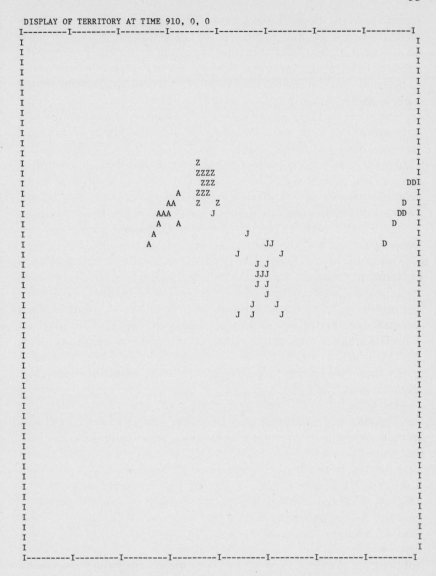

Fig. 8. *Territory Claimed by Lodges A.D. 910*

new lodge as close as possible in the same territory but at the unit
with the next highest elevation. In instances where a lodge is being
relocated and no acceptable new territory is found, subprogram
MOVE is called. This removes the WOMAN entity from the system
as if the inhabitants had moved from the locality to seek new land.
The units of territory they held are released to the system and their

lodge is abandoned. The release of territory, either through death of the owners or by emigration, is accomplished by subprogram RELE. RELE systematically removes each territorial unit from a LODGE entity and writes a message noting when the lodge was originally constructed, when abandoned, and the number of units of each resource zone type released to the system.

Subprogram HSIZ is included to allow for changes in family composition that necessitate increased house size. HSIZ has not been developed to its full potential for this program, but is included in this discussion to demonstrate the flexibility and possible realism to which such a simulation can be extended. The capability exists with HSIZ to provide a formulation for house size such as those offered by Naroll (1962) and Cook and Heizer (1968). There was no reason for using HSIZ here given the intent and untested nature of this program.

The subprograms for the addition of territory are simple in concept, but were moderately difficult to program. CLRTP (3065) initializes the amounts and types of territorial units for each lodge to zero. TRTYP (3100) determines the number of units of each resource zone necessary for each family; the number is based on family size, age composition, and whether or not the climatic change has occurred. Considerable flexibility exists in this subprogram for experimenting with the food requirement parameter in relation to the carrying capacity of the environment. Necessary territory is added to a lodge by searching the area around the lodge for unclaimed units. TRADD uses the information in TRTYP in its search procedures. The eight units contiguous to the unit in which the lodge is located are searched first and then the units around those eight and so on until the proper number of units of each type has been claimed or a radius of 2.5 miles has been reached. The 2.5 mile figure is an arbitrary limit of efficient accessibility to necessary resources. The overall search procedure could be likened to a wave action radiating out from a central point. As each unit is checked against the number of units of each type already claimed versus the number of each still needed, TRADD either adds that unit to the lodge's territory or rejects it. If a unit is unclaimed, it remains available to potential claim by another lodge. Because of this condition, the territories of lodges may be intermingled; this should be acceptable given the proximal matrilocality residence rule that implies some territory will overlap with that of close kin. It further allows for more efficient use of resources.

PWOMN is an output routine that prints information about each WOMAN entity and her attributes. It is not used to manipulate data, but plays an important role in verification and validation of the model.

Summary

The simular model developed to deal with changing settlement patterns was programmed for the computer in SIMSCRIPT, a FORTRAN-like language designed specifically for complex simulations. SIMSCRIPT uses defined entities and their attributes as the data base on which various manipulations operate. These operations occur through the actions of events, both endogenous and exogenous, on the system. Within these events, task-specific subprograms perform basic data manipulation. Glenwood I, the particular program for changing settlement patterns in the Glenwood locality, was composed of three major entities (WOMAN, MATRH, LODGE), three exogenous events (START, TRNS1, STOP), five endogenous events (SEASN, SNAP, MARY, BIRTH, DEATH), and several subprograms related to the location of a lodge and various output functions.

The programming was not particularly difficult in terms of syntax errors. However, it was very time-consuming and moderately costly. Elements that had not even been considered in the analysis stage of building the model had to be dealt with in the programming. Most of these elements related to establishing links between various subsystems. The major difficulties with the program were the logical errors, which were eliminated in the verification stage.

8.   Verification

The verification stage is the most demanding and potentially the most frustrating segment of the model building process. Verification is done for the purpose of determining the logical consistency of the model or, more simply put, to see if the model is behaving as the model builder intended. The tasks of this stage are discussed in more detail in Chapter 2. Verification for Glenwood I took approximately a year and some model segments could still be more adequately verified. Glenwood I did, however, appear to be performing consistently as anticipated. The major steps of verification of Glenwood I, with emphasis on the difficulties that are likely to appear in comparable total society simulations, are discussed below.

The importance of being able to monitor system status variables became evident almost immediately. It was simply inadequate to have only a final map or list of lodge locations printed at the end of the simulation runs. The model's complexity demanded more. To this end, monitoring devices were included when programming of the Glenwood I prototype began. Any time a WRITE statement appeared in the program list, a status variable was to be monitored. The SNAP event and PWOMN subprogram were likewise conceptualized to accomplish the same task. The role of these devices for verification is discussed for each major segment of the model and organized generally under the terms used in Chapter 6.

System Environment
The major problem of programming the environment and its links with the cultural system concerned the development of the "map" array that contained data on topography (elevation) and the resource zone code for each grid unit. These data were stored for retrieval in a simple external program called LOCAL that supposedly set up the grid units on an X-Y coordinate system to be used in the simulation. Within the simulation program itself there was no method to actually determine whether the data in the grid units were properly stored; the map printed in SNAP was merely a blank 50 by 80 grid on which the claimed territories were to be located, but there was no indication regarding the elevation or

96

resource type of the unit. Proper entry of these data is vital to the function of the program since subsistence and location are geared to resources and topography. The map was most quickly checked by requesting a printout of the data as stored in the array. Later, individual units of territory for each lodge were selected via subprogram TRADD to see if the units claimed were of the correct type and elevation. Once satisfied with the storage, these monitors were deleted from the program. Another problem with the environment concerned the climatic changes that occur through exogenous event TRNS1. The event was expected to change the oak-hickory forest zones above a certain elevation into hillslope grassland zones. Verification was accomplished in the same fashion as the original check of LOCAL by printing out the data array and comparing elevations and resource types from the array before and after TRNS1.

Population

The stochastic core of the model (the population subsystem of BIRTH, MARY, and DEATH) was expected to supply a body of individuals who would both use the environmental resources and locate new lodges. The life events were programmed to be carried out by random number generation in conjunction with a series of age-specific, cumulative probability life tables. As Mihram (1972a:628) suggests, verification of the stochastic models that use machine-generated random numbers is ultimately a verification of the system's random number generator itself. Being incapable of conducting such a verification, the veracity of the computer's random number generating devices must be assumed. A series of discussions concerning the actual nonrandom nature of machine-generated random numbers can be examined in Wyman (1970).

The nature of the use of life tables and random numbers for small populations presents potential problems. It is possible that a generation, upon reaching reproductive age, will not produce offspring, thereby bringing the population to extinction within a short time. Further, if one considers a small scale society to be endogamous, it is possible that there will be a paucity of socially acceptable potential matings at some time. This leads to a gradual decline in population and little chance exists that an adequate breeding population could be maintained for recovery. This problem in population is discussed by Wobst (1974), who solved it by using self-regulating life tables so that sex ratios, fertility rates, and mortality rates could change in order to maintain a minimum acceptable breeding population. In Glenwood I the problem was avoided by making the locality's inhabitants exogamous. Thus no mates need to be sought from within the locality's relatively small population pool. New mates are always considered available if the probabilities dictate marriage. The only potential difficulty for the system would occur if, during one generation, only male offspring were produced. There would be no females within the locality who could marry, locate a lodge, and produce new offspring, causing system collapse after a few years. During no run of the simulation did the entire population become exclusively male, although particular families did. The life tables and sex ratio used in the model are essentially idealized for a small scale society by Turner (n.d.) and were verified by him. Given these concerns for potential problems, the stochastic segment of the population system was considered to be behaving as anticipated and therefore verified. However, problems in specific structures of the population segment were discovered.

The probability of any one female having a child was expected to be greatest while she was in her mid-teens to her mid-twenties and to taper off to low probability by her late thirties. The original runs of the program demonstrated that the females were indeed fertile during the expected years, producing children during every three year interval. However, they did not taper off after they reached their mid-thirties and some were having children well past age fifty with the average number of offspring near fifteen. The BIRTH event was not functioning as expected or as the life tables indicated it should. The program was supposed to have decreased the probability of a female having a child if a child was born during the prior three year interval. This was to be done by decreasing the probability of another birth by 10%. Instead, the factor meant to decrease the probability was added to the existing probability and actually increased the probability of a woman having a child as she aged. If a woman had a child in the previous interval the likelihood of her having another in the next interval was increased about 70%. This problem was corrected easily once it was detected, but actually caused another. BIRTH also has the function of scheduling the next birth after a birth has occurred in a given interval. It was discovered via the PWOMN monitor that on occasion a woman would bear a child as late as five years after her death—an interesting medical phenomenon but a bit unrealistic. The problem was solved by the addition of a simple test of the woman's death date against the current system time in the BIRTH scheduling device. The behaviors of the population routines were sometimes frustrating and often amusing but not especially difficult to correct and verify.

Subsistence and Locational Rules

The subsistence system is incorporated into the model by each family's claim to certain numbers of resource zone units in the proximity of their lodge. It is carried out in subprogram TRADD. The technique is to determine the needs of the family in TRTYP and to claim the needed units by expanding systematically outward from the lodge location. Since the procedure is relatively complex, several diagnostics were added to aid in detecting and debugging problems. One diagnostic device is the SNAP map that displays territorial claims. Another device, the statements in TRADD, indicate when territory is added, the number of expansions to the 2.5 mile radius search limit, a list of each unit claimed by the X-Y coordinate, and a tabulation of the number of each type of resource unit needed and claimed by each lodge. With these devices, verifying the procedure was a simple matter of mapping out by hand the units claimed to see if the search procedure was acceptably followed. Only one problem appeared: the search procedure tended to "miss" needed units to the north of the lodge after the first outward expansion was made. In several runs the diagnostics indicated otherwise. The result was a movement out of the locality by several families since the needed resources were supposedly not available. This produced an artificially low population and number of lodges. Consequently, the search procedure was modified until it functioned properly and verified in the same way in which the original problem was detected. This problem solved, it was discovered that in subprogram CHECK, which calculates the acceptability of a potential territory, those units of territory not claimed by an existing lodge but within the radius created by their claimed units were not considered in calculation of the acceptability ratio. There was, in other words, no intermingling of territories even among kinsmen. This was not likely behavior in the real world nor was it efficient use of space and resources. Consequently, the subprogram was altered to provide for territorial intermingling.

The final problem caused a partial reanalysis of the locational rules in the original system. Upon conclusion of several runs of the simulation, as the locations of the simulated lodges were being plotted, it was noted that if two or more females from the same family married relatively close in time, the location of their lodges was the same. This behavior of the system was disconcerting since the anticipated pattern was a relatively dispersed one. The behavior should not produce a clustered pattern until after the climatic change, and it was expected that a lodge would claim as territory the unit in which it was located. That location would thereby be impossible for another lodge to claim. When this heavy use of one unit occurred, the territories of each lodge in the cluster were examined carefully. It was discovered that each lodge had the proper number and composition of resource zone units and that the unit in which the lodges were located was, indeed, unclaimed by any one of the lodges. Reanalysis of the LGLOC subprogram showed that the lodge location had nothing to do with the particular territorial units claimed except that it be located in a unit of the ecotone type and at the highest elevation within the square formed by the territory. Some of those units are not actually claimed by a lodge. Given the possibilities of territorial intermingling, the rule of proximal matrilocality, and extremely abundant territory in an area, it was possible and indeed probable that some lodges would be located within the same unit at approximately the same time. It was determined that this could happen in reality given adequate resources; therefore the program was not changed. This was an instance of "serendipity" occurring from simulation as discussed by Thomas (1972).

Summary

A series of devices was included in the synthesis of Glenwood I that would allow the status of the system to be easily monitored. These devices include TRACE, SNAP, PWOMN, and a series of simple WRITE statements. In this way, relatively simple tests could be performed to determine whether the system was behaving as anticipated in the analysis and synthesis stages of model building. A number of problems were located and corrected in the environmental, population, and locational rule components of the program. It is not known whether all logical errors were located; it is assumed that they were. The probability exists that a unique initialization or situation created from the stochastic segments of the model might pinpoint new problems. This may be possible since only one random number stream was used during verification.

9. Validation and Initial Inferences

Just as the verification stage in a model's development serves as a check on the system synthesis stage, the validation stage is undertaken to check the systems analysis stage (see Fig. 1). Validation is accomplished by comparing responses from the verified model with the corresponding responses or measurements from the actual modelled system (Mihram 1972a:628). Under ideal circumstances experimentation is conducted with both the model and modelled system. The operating conditions of the modelled system are set for a fixed duration and the results recorded. The corresponding environmental conditions and a comparable time period are then set for the model. The results are recorded and compared on a one-to-one basis with the results of the actual system. With deterministic models the comparisons are relatively simple; with formalized stochastic models validation by comparison becomes a statistical matter as in the verification stage. The statistical procedures that are most efficacious remain a matter of concern for statisticians (Mihram 1972a:628).

These experimentation and formalized validation procedures cannot normally be accomplished for archaeological problems that have focused on extinct systems such as the one under consideration here. Nor would there be particular utility in such experimentation and validation given the rough estimations in the systems analysis stage. Further, and perhaps most important, the results of the modelled system are not necessarily complete and the known settlement distribution may also be incomplete. Comparison of the results of the simulated system to the actual system would therefore limit the use of formal validation. Some alternative informal validation could very well give information that will pinpoint weaknesses in the systems analysis stage so that the model could be restructured and brought within tolerable range of the known system. As Pool (1967:57) pointed out, the value of a total society simulation is not necessarily limited in usefulness by the limitations of the data on which it is based or by its level of reality. These factors in mind, an informal validation procedure was developed for the Glenwood I model. Limited inferences were drawn from these procedures and modifications were made in the model. It should

101

always be remembered that the inferences drawn entail considerable risk since no formal validation can be accomplished.

Informal Validation Procedures for Glenwood I

Only the most naive hope was retained for a one-to-one correspondence of simulated to real lodges; achieving that correspondence would badly cheat probability. The original assumptive bases included similarity of modern to prehistoric environment, extremely generalized demographic models, and an assumed 400 year duration. Each would be adequate to skew the simulated lodges from the real pattern. All three, along with many other lesser assumptions, might well synergize to produce a pattern vastly different from the known settlement distribution.

Recognizing these possibilities and their frustrating consequences allows a certain "playful" attitude to develop in the model builder. Perfection is not likely to be achieved; therefore, the concern must be with the amount of information that can be gleaned from the model. The immediate problem is to see if the model can generate a pattern close to the real distribution. If the model is not close enough to satisfy, changes must be made beginning at the systems analysis level by either altering parameters or by restructuring certain segments of the system. Several such alterations are likely to be made; the problem then becomes a matter of determining which of the altered models generates a pattern closest to the known distribution.

There are essentially two ways to determine which model produces the "best" fit: visual inspection and statistical measures. Human visual capacities allow very accurate impressions to be formed if two or more patterns are vastly different. Obvious differences can be easily seen if, for instance, the model prevents spread of settlement into a certain area while in reality settlement did develop in that area. Visual inspection allows generalized comparisons for purposes of gross sorting to the extent that the results are nearly 100% replicable. However, in cases where two patterns are only slightly different, visual inspection has limited utility and replicability suffers. This problem, compounded by multiple comparisons and the need to rank the patterns by their closeness to reality, causes the difficulties of replicability to become acute. At this point a statistic can aid in the comparative process and increase replicability. The selection of a statistic remains. Many are potentially useful, but there are differences in the ease of application.

The primary concern in the problem of Glenwood locality

settlement was the nature of the settlement distribution. Did two distinct patterns, dispersed and nucleated, exist? A measure that considered this question could be useful. It could be applied to both the real distribution and each simulated distribution and the results compared. In this way a meaningless and complicated process of one-to-one lodge comparison could be avoided.

The measure selected was a simple statistic called the Coefficient of Dispersion (CD). Thomas (1973:163) effectively used the statistic in his BASIN I simulation to compare real and simulated distributions of several artifact classes. CD is defined by Sokal and Rohlf (1969:88) as a ratio of the variance to the mean of points distributed over a sampling grid: $CD = s^2/\overline{Y}$. A CD value less than one indicates a more dispersed (more random) distribution while a value greater than one indicates a more clustered (less random) distribution. Essentially, the statistic is a measure of a sample's (Poisson) distribution in space. The question being considered by CD clustering or anticlustering of a population in space is similar to that asked in Nearest Neighbor analysis. The Nearest Neighbor method measures the deviation of the distribution of a population in space from a random distribution toward an anticlustered or clustered pattern (Washburn 1974:322). The CD was simpler to apply and it was adequate for purposes noted above; it was selected on that basis.

The Coefficient of Dispersion for either the real or simulated distribution of lodges in the Glenwood locality was calculated by plotting the lodge locations on a base map and imposing on it a grid of 40 units (5 x 8); each unit represented one square mile. The frequency of lodges for each grid unit was determined. The mean, the variance, and their ratio were then calculated. The resulting CD for the known distribution was 3.76, indicating a clustered pattern (Fig. 9). It can be assumed that the closer the CD of the simulated pattern to the 3.76 of the real pattern, the greater the likelihood of the model's validity. Since the statistic simply measures dispersion and nucleation, it is possible that an entirely different distribution from reality could yield a similar CD to the real distribution. It therefore becomes necessary to combine the use of CD with visual inspection to determine the "best" fit.

These informal validation procedures were applied to all runs of the simulation. Each run of the simulation, the results of the validation procedures, and preliminary inferences based on visual inspection of the distribution produced by each run are discussed below. Even though the CD is discussed for each run, it was not applied in reality until all runs were completed.

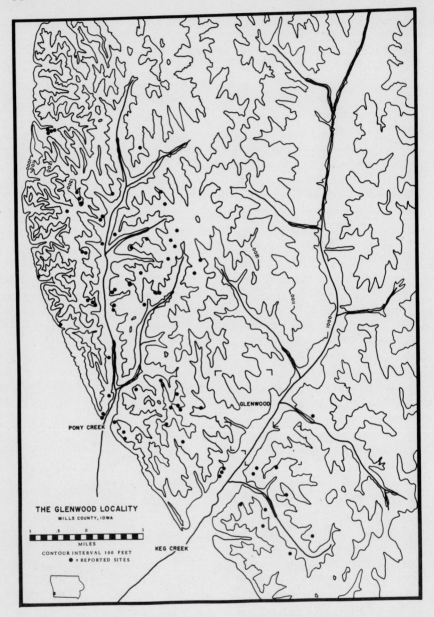

Fig. 9. *Known Distribution of Earthlodges in the Glenwood Locality*

System Simulation

The following descriptions of the seven runs of the simulation must be prefaced by comments on how each run was accomplished. The system synthesis stage sets the programming only. It does not provide the system with an initial state or data set on which the rules of the system operate. This initialization is done by the model builder. Glenwood I initialization primarily includes the locations of pioneer settlements and the structure of the family residing in each lodge. Family information includes the birth dates of the mates and the sex and birth dates of any children. Formal initialization includes the life tables for the demographic component of the model. The model's exogenous events are also given a date for occurrence. For Glenwood I these include a date for each stage of the climatic change (TRNS1) and dates that give the duration of the run, i.e., the dates for the start and finish of the system. An example of an initialization is included in the Appendix. In addition to the formal initialization, the parameters for various parts of the model are set. The necessary territorial requirements for each individual or family in the system are determined by adjusting statements in subprogram TRTYP. Any desired alterations in locational rules (e.g., elevation parameters) can be made in subprogram LGLOC. If changes are desired in any other parameters they can be set by altering the appropriate subprogram or event. Several of these alterations, both in the formal initialization and in the subprograms, were made during the runs of Glenwood I.

Run A incorporated all the variables discussed in the systems analysis stage and programmed in the synthesis stage. It is, in effect, the test of the various hypotheses offered concerning Glenwood locality settlement *as structured in this model.* The run was scheduled to last 400 simulated years from A.D. 900 to A.D. 1300. The assumed length of occupation in the locality by Central Plains tradition peoples was derived from radiocarbon dates available from the locality at the time programming was done. The dates range from A.D. 870 to A.D. 1260, a span of approximately 400 years disregarding the standard deviation. These dates have been a source of contention, but they were supported (see Zimmerman 1971:19-21) and therefore used to set the temporal parameters for this run. The climatic changes (TRNS1) were set to occur at two points in time, A.D. 1150 and A.D. 1180, reducing the available units of the oak-hickory forest resource zone. It should be noted that for all runs the important factors are not the precise calendric dates themselves, but rather the time span covered and the locations of particular events within that span.

At this point one can only speculate on the size of the group involved in pioneer settlement. That initial settlement was not large was assumed. Four lodges were initialized in Pony Creek locations. Each was inhabited by a mated couple; three of the couples had female children. Each adult was allotted one unit each of oak-hickory forest, forest-grassland ecotone, and hillslope grassland, and each lodge was allotted one unit of stream bottomland. Since it was assumed that horticulture was not heavily practiced at this time, only one unit of stream bottomland was necessary for each lodge to have access to water or practice limited gardening. It should again be noted that each unit of territory equals 6.4 acres.

Figure 10 is the plotted distribution of lodges according to the structure of the model and initialization as generated in Run A. By a simple visual inspection, it is apparent that the pattern is very highly clustered, especially in the area near the southernmost tributary of Pony Creek. Comparison of this distribution to the real distribution adequately demonstrates the clustering. The Coefficient of Dispersion for Run A is 14.81; this is vastly greater than the 3.76 calculated for the real distribution and confirms visual inspection. To a great extent, this large difference is a function of the number of lodges produced in Run A. The 138 lodges is more than double the lodges of the real distribution. Also, a more detailed visual inspection shows that there is no spread of lodges into the Keg Creek valley, while the real distribution shows several lodges in that drainage.

Analysis of lodge location and territorial allocation over the 400 year span of the run indicates that no population pressure on the environmental carrying capacity occurred. The limited nature of territorial requirements would not necessarily stress the environment if population levels were low. An examination of the population levels of the locality demonstrated that this was the case. Figure 11 is a population curve for the locality over the 400 years. The frequencies were calculated by assuming that all female children were permanent residents of the locality. As they married, the husband was added to the total and continued to be counted until his death. Male children were counted as residents only until their marriage. The population for the locality never exceeds 80 contemporaneous individuals, a population density smaller than three persons per square mile.

Given the low population density and low territorial requirements, no pressure on carrying capacity ever appears. The reduction of oak-hickory forest units with the onset of the climatic change has no impact on settlement that is readily perceptible. It is not necessary

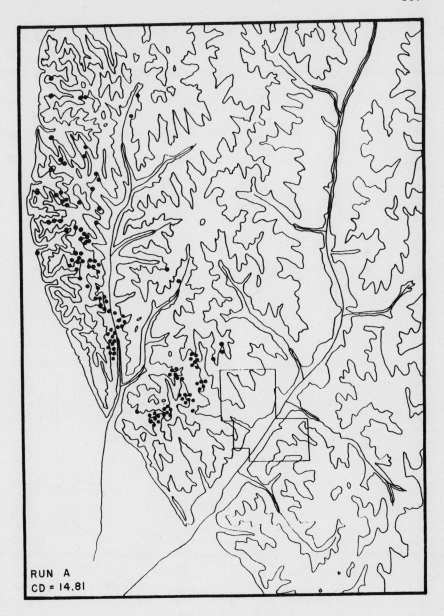

Fig. 10. *Simulated Distribution of Earthlodges: Run A*

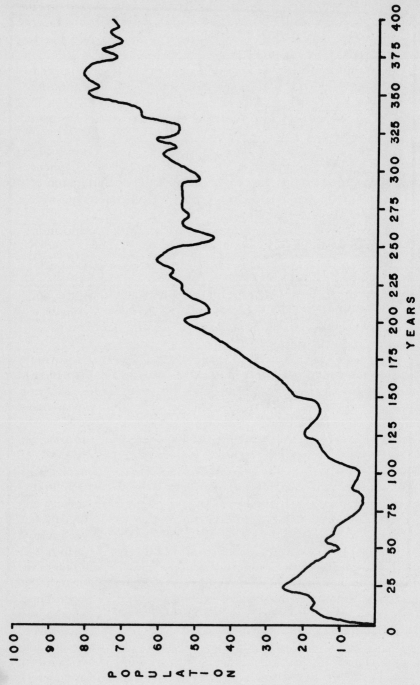

Fig. 11. *Population Curve: Run A*

for families to either leave the locality or shift toward greater dependence on kinsmen due to population pressure on resources. This is further substantiated by the lack of spread into the Keg Creek drainage, which has its own available resources.

Based on the results described above, the following inferences could explain the variability of Run A from the known distribution:

1) The temporal span is too long, allowing the development of too many lodges.

2) The territorial requirements are too small. Increasing requirements could result in greater spread of settlement into areas such as Keg Creek valley for better utilization of resources. This could place stress on the environment with the onset of climatic changes.

3) The population tables do not allow significant population levels to be reached.

4) The initial population of the locality is larger than assumed.

5) Other problems could exist in the model that are not immediately visible; random factors could play a role, or a combination of several of the above factors could occur.

These limited inferences from the results of Run A provide a baseline for experimentation in Runs B through G. Discussion of initialization, results, and inferences for those runs are only minimally detailed with the exception of Run G in which major model changes were made.

Run B was initialized exactly as Run A except the run time was reduced to 300 years and territorial requirements were altered. All resource zone requirements were doubled to two units for each adult and each child under 12 years of age was allotted one unit of each resource type. Again, one unit of stream bottomland was allotted per lodge. With the additional requirement for children, necessary territory was more than doubled. These changes reduced the number of earthlodges from the 138 of Run A to 84, which is 19 more than the 65 of the known distribution. Visual inspection of the distribution in Run B (Fig. 12) shows a less clustered pattern than in Run A but still more clustered than the real pattern. A Coefficient of Dispersion of 8.45 confirms visual inspection (3.76 for the real distribution). Analysis of the distribution shows only a limited spread into the Keg Creek valley. Again, population levels remain low, comparable to Run A. Over the 300 year span, heavy reuse of territory occurs, which low population would allow. Consequently,

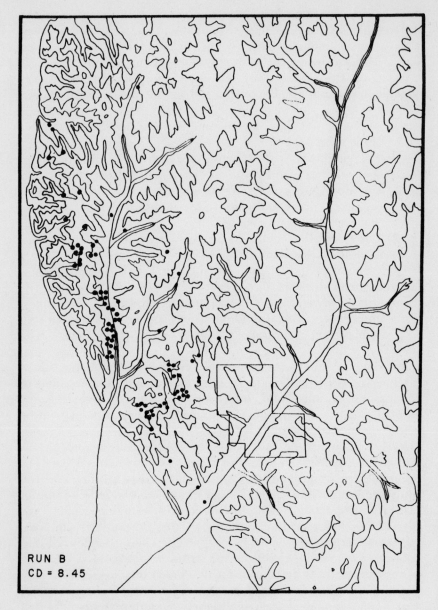

RUN B
CD = 8.45

Fig. 12. *Simulated Distribution of Earthlodges: Run B*

as in Run A, the climatic change has no impact. It was inferred that the territorial requirements were too large. This, combined with low population, may have caused the heavy reuse. This in turn could result in the more clustered pattern. Run time appears to be the factor most responsible for the reduction in number of lodges.

Run C tested the impact of run time on the system. The span was 425 years, an increase of 125 years over Run B. The climatic change was totally removed. Territorial requirements were reduced from Run B levels to one unit of each resource zone per individual (including children). As in Runs A and B, one unit of bottomland was allotted per lodge. Initialization was modified slightly by placing one lodge near Keg Creek to test the impact of initial location changes on the system.

The map of settlement distribution produced in Run C (Fig. 13) demonstrates that 205 lodges were generated. This is vastly more than the known lodge number of 65. On visual inspection the lodges appear very clustered, especially along Pony Creek. The Coefficient of Dispersion of 13.80 indicates that Run C settlement is less clustered than Run A (14.81), but far more clustered than the real distribution. The clustered effect is slightly ameliorated by the spread of lodges into the northern portions of the Keg Creek drainage, a pattern that is not known to exist in reality. The additional run time probably had the greatest impact on the system by allowing an extra generation of females to marry and reproduce. The absence of a climatic change and the low territorial requirements facilitated settlement spread into areas outside Pony Creek valley. The spread into the northern reaches of Keg Creek was partly caused by the elimination of climatic change. The climatic change reduces oak-hickory forest at the higher elevations. Since the northern part of the locality is higher in elevation than most other areas, oak-hickory units would remain and could be used late in the run given population pressure on resources to the south. At any rate, a pattern was produced in Run C that is very different from the known settlement pattern.

Run D was reduced by 75 years to a duration of 350 years because of the large number of lodges produced in Runs A and C. The climatic change was reinstated and the territorial requirements of Run A were reestablished. Initialization was the same as that of Run A with four lodges. The major change was a shift in locational rules in subprogram LGLOC. In effect, this change forced those constructing new lodges after the onset of climatic change to locate at lower elevations. No longer would the highest elevation be selected; the lodge could be located lower than 1050 feet in the unit

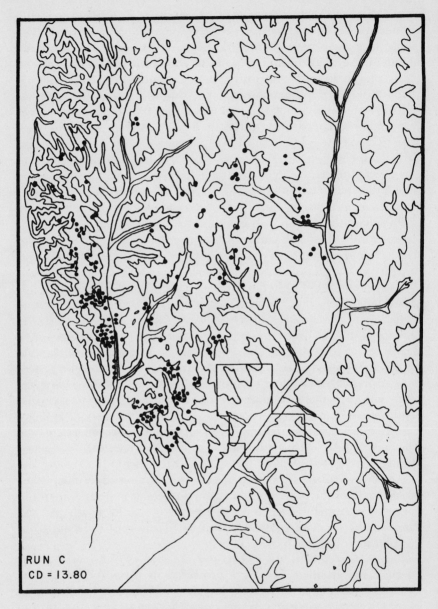

RUN C
CD = 13.80

Fig. 13. *Simulated Distribution of Earthlodges: Run C*

of territory no matter what kind of resource zone was nearest the center of the territory claimed by the lodge. This would, in effect, force locational change that was to have occurred naturally as a result of the climatic shift. Figure 14 shows the results of this run. Ninety-eight lodges were produced, which is only 33 more than the known number. Again, the pattern is very clustered and the Coefficient of Dispersion (18.77) is high. The pattern is visually similar to real settlement, especially in the area between Pony and Keg Creeks. Keg Creek drainage still has virtually no settlement, and a very large cluster of lodges (15) exists on Pony Creek. The cluster is similarly located but much larger than the known pattern of lodges. Finally, lodges are often located at lower elevations that are nearer the bluffs but on the floodplain of the Missouri River; these locations are not known in reality. The artificiality of choosing a lower elevation after climatic change, even though it is similar to other locational rules, is bothersome in that it affects only new lodges and not lodges that already exist in the system.

Run E lasted 375 simulated years. The territorial units required for subsistence were returned to the level of Run B: two units of each research zone per adult, one per child, and one unit of stream bottomland per lodge. The climatic change was deleted. The locational rules were the same as those of Run D except that the shift to lower elevation was not keyed to climatic change. Lodges built after A.D. 1150 were arbitrarily located at an elevation lower than 1050 feet in the unit nearest the center of a lodge's territory. Because the climatic change was eliminated, the number of available resource units of oak-hickory forest was high. The concern in this run was the impact of "random" factors influencing the locational decisions.

Run E produced 122 lodges, nearly double those known. The distribution of these lodges (Fig. 15) is similar to that of Run D with lodges out in the floodplain and little spread into Keg Creek. The distribution is still clustered, but the Coefficient of Dispersion of 7.60 is reduced from that of Run D. This reduction is primarily a result of the dispersed nature of settlement in the northern part of the Pony Creek drainage and floodplain settlement. Several clusters of five or more lodges exist that are not known to exist in reality. No pressure for territory occurs until the last five years of the run, but there is still little spread into Keg Creek valley.

Run F was reduced to 300 years and the climatic change was reinstated. Territorial requirements were the same as in Run E. Again, four lodges provided initial settlement. Sixty-six lodges were produced during this run, only one more than known in reality.

114

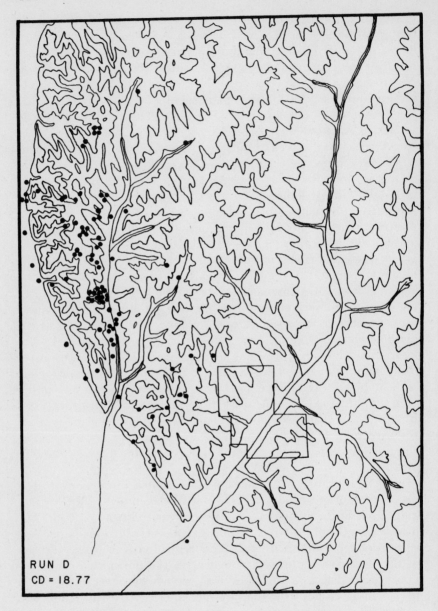

Fig. 14. *Simulated Distribution of Earthlodges: Run D*

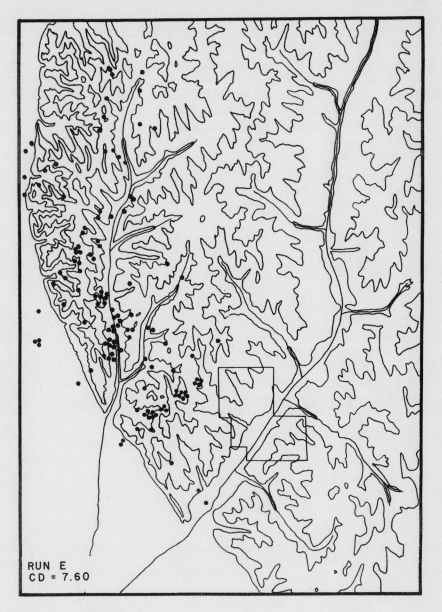

RUN E
CD = 7.60

Fig. 15. *Simulated Distribution of Earthlodges: Run E*

Figure 16 shows that the lodges were very clustered, more so than the known pattern. This was confirmed by a Coefficient of Dispersion of 8.39. Also, several large clusters were produced in the area between Pony and Keg Creeks that do not exist in the known distribution. Again, Keg Creek valley has little settlement. The reduced number of lodges appears to be primarily a function of reduced time, low population, and large subsistence requirements. The impact of climatic change is negligible.

Run G provides an interesting contrast to the previous runs. Runs A through F represented the particular line of reasoning that the length of occupation in the Glenwood locality was at least 300 years and that pioneer settlement was limited. With the exception of Run F, the settlement patterns that were generated produced many more lodges than were known to have existed in reality. Further, and more important, all the model-generated patterns were extremely clustered; their Coefficients of Dispersion were 7.60 or higher compared to a CD of 3.76 for the real pattern. Run E, which produced the lowest Coefficient of Dispersion (7.60), had other notable problems, including several lodges located on the Missouri River floodplain. Consequently, the duration of Run G was drastically reduced. As discussed by Zimmerman (1971), a number of radiocarbon dates from the locality do fall within a 150 year period. Run time was therefore set at 150 years for Run G. Climatic change was eliminated since it had insignificant impact on settlement in the previous runs. Territorial requirements were set high at two units each of oak-hickory forest, forest-grassland ecotone, and hillslope grassland per adult; one unit of each per child; and one unit of stream bottomland per lodge. Another major change in Run G was the doubling of initial lodges to eight with an increased initial population of 22. Locations of pioneer lodges were scattered throughout the locality with two in the Keg Creek drainage.

The number of lodges produced was 97, the lowest total except for Run F and 32 more than the known distribution. Visual inspection shows a pattern only slightly more clustered than the real pattern. The Coefficient of Dispersion is 6.69, the lowest produced by any run. Visually, the major difference between Run G and the others is the spread of lodges throughout the southern part of the Keg Creek drainage. Although settlement on Keg Creek is slightly more dense, the general simulated locations are similar to real lodge locations (Fig. 17).

The lodge distribution in Run G exhibits some deficiencies when visually compared to the known pattern. The lodges in the area between Keg and Pony Creeks appear to be more highly clustered

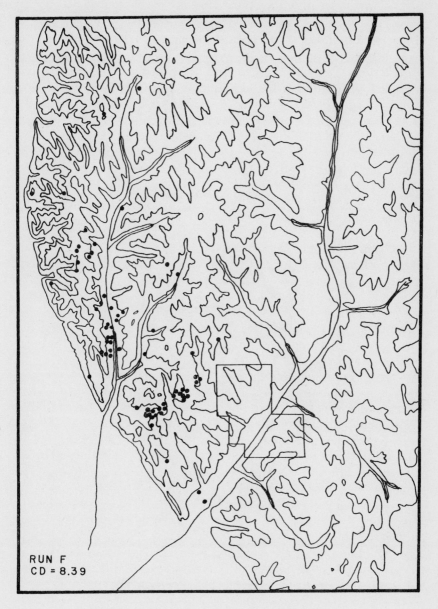

RUN F
CD = 8.39

Fig. 16. *Simulated Distribution of Earthlodges: Run F*

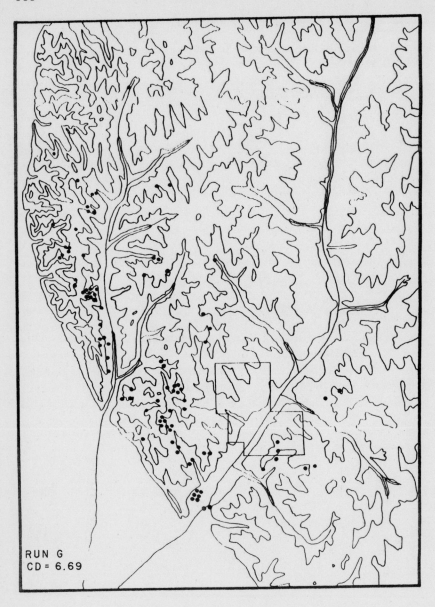

RUN G
CD = 6.69

Fig. 17. *Simulated Distribution of Earthlodges: Run G*

than in the real distribution. Clusters appear that are slightly larger than any known cluster. The hollows opening onto the Missouri River floodplain are less intensively occupied at lower elevations than in the real distribution. Finally, the area immediately east of the central portion of the Pony Creek drainage is not as heavily occupied as in reality.

Population in the locality is slightly greater for Run G than for Run A. Figure 18 is the population curve for Run G. The maximum population reached is 100 individuals, which is 20 more than that produced in the 400 year span. The less clustered effect of the lodges results from a combination of the low population density, the high territorial requirements, and a short run time, which leaves little time or need for reuse of territory. The initialization of two lodges in the Keg Creek drainage appears to be partially responsible for the increased number of lodges in that area.

As a final experiment the data provided by Run G were manipulated. If a run time of 150 years produced a reasonably acceptable distribution, a further reduction to 100 years might prove to be even more acceptable. Consequently, the lodges that had been produced in the Run G simulation by year 100 were plotted (Fig. 19) and their Coefficient of Dispersion computed. The resulting CD of 5.23 was between the 6.69 of Run G and the 3.76 of the real distribution. The number of lodges produced by year 100 was 65, exactly the number known for the locality. Even so, the distribution of these lodges is slightly more clustered. Visually, some of the larger clusters have disappeared, especially near the opening of Keg Creek valley onto the Missouri River floodplain and in the area between Keg and Pony Creeks.

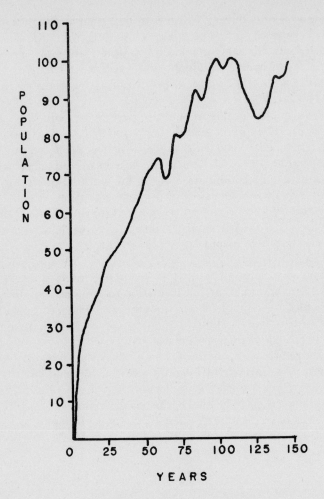

Fig. 18. *Population Curve: Run G*

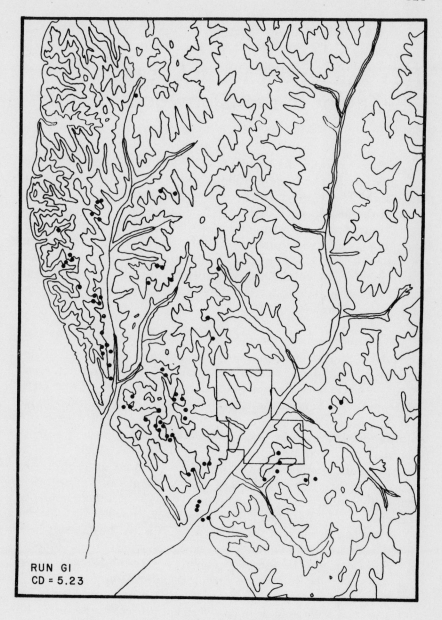

RUN GI
CD = 5.23

Fig. 19. *Simulated Distribution of Earthlodges: Run G1*

10. Inferences about Locational Behavior in the Glenwood Locality

The process of inferring locational behaviors in a general way from a rather specific set of propositions and conditions is a precarious operation. This is especially the case when one cannot experiment with both the model and the modelled system and when formal validation cannot be accomplished (Mihram 1972a:628). Further, "simulations can prove nothing about prehistory" (Mosimann and Martin 1975:313). They can only show that given certain assumptions and conditions, a particular model is feasible. With these *caveats* in mind, several inferences can be made from the simulations described in Chapter 9.

Climatic Change

Anderson and Zimmerman (n.d.) proposed that a climatic change from the cool, moist Neo-Atlantic episode to the warmer, drier Pacific episode was a major cause for the shift from dispersed to nucleated settlement in the Glenwood locality. Climatic change had only minimal impact on the settlement systems in all runs of the simulation. Given the low population density, a maximum population ca. 100 individuals, and even extremely high territorial requirements, population pressure was not placed on the carrying capacity of the environment. The climatic change did not cause a major disequilibrium in the subsistence system such that adaptation was necessary in the settlement system. Several possibilities exist that could explain the lack of disequilibrium. The first has already been noted: the low population levels never approach environmental carrying capacity. The second possibility is that the climatic change did not occur at all. If it occurred, its impact on the Glenwood locality was less severe than in other areas of the Central Plains. The effect of the Pacific episode on the fauna of the locality was evidently not major if Johnson (1972) is correct in his interpretations. Even if the climatic change was generally severe, it is possible that the rugged local topography acted as an effective climatic buffer (Asch et al. 1972:24). That climatic change had any impact must remain problematic. That climatic change might have had any important effects on cultures in the area has been noted by Butzer (1973) in his review of Henning's (1968, 1969) *Climatic Change and the Mill Creek Culture of Iowa, Pts. I & II.* He says, ". . . the ecological response to environmental change remains vague and somewhat conjectural at the site-specific level and enigmatic at the regional level" (Butzer 1973:254). His comments must apply as well to Nebraska phase sites in Iowa.

Questions can be raised concerning assumptions made in the model, particularly the demographic considerations, the similarity of prehistoric and historic natural environments, and the level of dependence of the peoples on hunting and gathering. Recognizing these weaknesses, it can be inferred that within the structure and parameters of this model the climatic change had virtually no impact on the locational behaviors or decisions of the individuals living in the locality.

Dispersed versus Nucleated Settlement

One of the original intentions of this study was to determine whether Glenwood locality settlement was dispersed, nucleated, or some combination and how such a pattern might have developed. Except for Run G, all runs of the simulation produced clusters of more than ten earthlodges. Run G produced no cluster larger than nine lodges and its shorter version, Run G1, produced no cluster larger than four lodges. Hamlets of two to ten lodges, as defined by Wood (1969:105), do exist, while no villages of ten or more lodges are known to have actually existed. In this model, clusters result from sisters locating themselves very close to each other and their parents or use of approximately the same site at a later date. Consequently, it is possible that contemporaneity of lodges in the small clusters could be demonstrated by dating techniques or by discovery of sherds from the same vessel in two or more lodges located near each other. In larger clusters, one would expect to find several contemporary lodges as well as some from an earlier or later period. Isolated homesteads appear to be the prevalent form of settlement in Run G with at least half the lodges separated from the others. That the model used in Run G came close to the real distribution is an indication that many isolated lodges or extremely small clusters (two to three lodges) can be generated within the suggested hypothetical framework for Central Plains tradition settlement systems. This does not necessarily negate Gradwohl's (1969) contention that the dispersed pattern is an artifact of survey

124

techniques, selective excavation, and site numbering practices. The universe of sites is not known for either the Glenwood locality or any other Central Plains tradition locality. Indeed, large clusters of lodges have been reported from the Glenwood locality by amateurs and construction personnel; none has yet been substantiated. This model suggests that if large clusters exist they are the result of sisters living in the same area or use by other groups at other times, but there were never more than four to five contemporary lodges. Glenwood I results cannot support Gradwohl's contention that the dispersed pattern is not the predominant form, at least for the Glenwood locality.

Population Levels

The generalized demographic model used in Glenwood I suggests that population levels in the Glenwood locality, no matter what the length of occupation, were low, rarely exceeding 100 contemporary individuals. To be sure, the model used is hardly above criticism. It is likely that a larger initial population would have produced a larger population. Larger pioneer settlement is not likely, however, since it would imply full-scale migration into the area. It is possible that the Glenwood locality pioneer settlement resulted from the fission of a community located in eastern Nebraska. Locality exogamy further acts to maintain a slow growth and to keep population levels low. Wedel (1961:95) suggested that Upper Republican and Nebraska communities seldom exceeded 50 or 100 individuals. Wood (1969:106) suggests that the small number of houses in a hamlet may be deceptive by analogy to historic groups since some lodges may house many more than ten persons. He further suggested that a household might contain extended families consisting of independent polygynous families.

The model used here suggests that these reconstructions are inadequate for the Glenwood locality. If one considers the Glenwood locality at any point in time as a single dispersed community, then Wedel's population estimates could be considered accurate. Applied to any hamlet, the estimates would be far too large.

The settlement distribution can be accomplished by using nuclear families or small extended families (husband, wife, children, wife's parents). Given this model and its population sizes, the nuclear family seems a more realistic structure. Rarely in a nuclear family would population exceed ten individuals. If only ten of these lodges were contemporaneous, they would comprise the 100 maximum population. Further, given the generally smaller floor area of the Glenwood lodges (400 to 1600 square feet compared to perhaps

2500 square feet for historic counterparts), the probable population differences in housing capabilities become apparent. In effect, it can be inferred from the Glenwood I model and its parameters that the population levels were generally smaller than has been suggested for the Glenwood locality and its Central Plains tradition contemporaries.

Time Span

The temporal span of occupation of Central Plains tradition peoples in the Glenwood locality has been a matter of controversy. Anderson (1961), using a seriation to build a sequence of sites in the locality, suggested an early end for his sequence at A.D. 800. He based this date on the affinity of some Glenwood ceramics to Upper Republican ceramics and an Upper Republican radiocarbon date of A.D. 800. Brown (1967), in his excavations on Pony Creek, determined the first four radiocarbon dates for the locality (Table 6). All but one were in the A.D. 1200 to A.D. 1290 range. The one remaining date, A.D. 900±90, was rejected as too early (Brown 1967:48). Brown generally criticized Anderson's sequence as starting too early. Zimmerman (1971) reevaluated Anderson's local sequence and Brown's critique and included six additional radiocarbon dates. Two early dates, A.D. 885±105 and A.D. 920±130, were from a single lodge. Another lodge had both an early date of A.D. 870±95 and a later date of A.D. 1260±100. A third lodge had a single plausible date of A.D. 1215±95 and a date of A.D. 430±100 that was disregarded. On the basis of the four early dates, two from a single lodge, Zimmerman (1971:20) chose to assume a 400 year period of occupation for the Glenwood locality.

That assumption provided the 400 year run time used in Run A of the simulation, which produced many more lodges than were known for the locality. The best correspondence was produced with a run time of 100 to 150 years. Thus it can be inferred that the locality was occupied for a considerably shorter duration than previously suggested. Even Brown (1967:73) hypothesized a span of 300 years (A.D. 1150 to A.D. 1450) for the locality.

Recent radiocarbon dates from the locality tend to corroborate the short duration of occupation. Twenty-six new dates have been added to the prior dates (John Hotopp, personal communication). All available dates are listed in Table 6. Given the standard deviation, 25 of the 36 dates fall within the 150 year interval between A.D. 1075 and A.D. 1225.

Table 6. *Radiocarbon Dates from the Glenwood Locality*

13ML216	A.D. 1200 ± 90*
13ML222	A.D. 1210 ± 80*
13ML219	A.D. 1280 ± 70*
	A.D. 900 ± 90
13ML119	A.D. 885 ± 105
	A.D. 920 ± 130
13ML121	A.D. 870 ± 95
	A.D. 1260 ± 100*
13ML124	A.D. 1215 ± 95*
	A.D. 430 ± 100
13ML126	A.D. 1220 ± 55*
	A.D. 965 ± 45
	A.D. 1110 ± 60*
13ML128	A.D. 1130 ± 50*
	A.D. 1160 ± 50*
	A.D. 1095 ± 55*
13ML129	A.D. 1130 ± 55*
	A.D. 1185 ± 55*
	A.D. 1125 ± 60*
13ML130	A.D. 1235 ± 90*
	A.D. 1005 ± 100*
	A.D. 1185 ± 110*
13ML132	A.D. 1640 ± 60
	A.D. 1090 ± 55*
	A.D. 1590 ± 55
13ML135	A.D. 975 ± 60
	A.D. 1040 ± 60*
	A.D. 1090 ± 60*
13ML136	A.D. 1075 ± 60*
	A.D. 1260 ± 50*
	A.D. 1085 ± 55*
	A.D. 1175 ± 55*
13ML138	A.D. 940 ± 55
13ML139	A.D. 1510 ± 45
	A.D. 1100 ± 55*
	A.D. 1115 ± 55*

*Given standard deviation, dates fall within 150 year interval between A.D. 1075 and A.D. 1225.

Summary

In general, if the results of this model are acceptable, Glenwood I demonstrates that a satisficing model is adequate to produce an approximation of the known Central Plains tradition settlement pattern in the Glenwood locality. The individuals who built the lodges had a set of biological needs and culturally defined desires that formed the core of the locational rules used in this simulation. Choice depended not on an optimal solution to the particular problem of location in an economic sense, but on satisfaction of particular needs given a limited set of alternatives and the operation of random factors. No particular natural environmental problem forced a new adaptation or a shift of priorities in the factors involved in decision making. Consequently, the location rules were applied consistently through time. Several factors interacted to produce a set of satisfactory locations that fulfilled needs; from this set a single lodge location was selected.

These inferences were based on the seven runs carried out as experiments. While these may be adequate to support the archaeological inferences drawn, more experimentation might have been appropriate. Primarily due to expense, little effort was made to test the model's behaviors with multiple runs that used a different random stream while holding all other variables constant. Such lack of experimentation could cause major problems either by obscuring certain important behaviors or by emphasizing relatively unimportant ones. Further explorations may alter some of the inferences or more firmly support others.

11. The Efficacy of Simulating Locational Processes

The simulation of locational processes in the Glenwood I model went through several cycles of revision and calibration. A model was produced that generated earthlodge locations similar to those known in reality for the Glenwood locality. This model was actually more simplistic than the original set of hypotheses offered by Anderson and Zimmerman (n.d.) to explain the development of settlement in the locality.

The model that produced the best results was one of short term cultural stability. The locality was inhabited by a relatively large number of persons (ca. 20) as pioneers; their lodges were dispersed throughout the locality. As the population grew, newly married females and their mates from outside the locality selected new lodge sites. These lodges were established according to the following general rules:

1) Enough territory of particular resource types must be available to practice a subsistence pattern dependent on hunting and gathering and, to some extent, horticulture.
2) Given there is ample territory of particular resource types, the lodge site must be as close as possible to the bride's parents.
3) The lodge location must be at the highest possible elevation given (1) and (2) above.

This pattern continued for 100 to 150 years. Population levels remained moderately low at no more than 100 individuals. The major factor determining location was not, as originally anticipated, the climatic change. There was no one causal factor determining the settlement pattern; it resulted from the interaction of several factors including demography (especially population and sex ratio), resource availability, and time.

Glenwood I has a number of weaknesses that must be considered when evaluating the conclusions drawn in Chapter 10. It is not a particularly realistic model. The demographic data were generalized

128

from small scale societies. More specific, but unavailable, life tables for the Glenwood locality could have drastically altered the model's outcome. These data could have made the model more realistic without increasing complexity. The same is true of the natural environmental information that is especially important in terms of resource zone territory allocations. Analogy from present to past environment may not necessarily hold. Actual prehistoric environmental information could have increased reality and not complexity. Resource zone units of 6.4 acres are relatively large and do not allow much flexibility or sensitivity to individual family needs. Smaller units would have drastically increased the size and complexity of an already large data set. Analysis of nutritional requirements per individual in relation to territorial allocation would have been useful, but would again markedly increase the model's complexity. Finally, more information concerning climatic change could have made a difference. The precise way in which climatic change affects a particular locality was only generally modelled.

The major weakness of Glenwood I is that it attempts to model a cognitive process in terms of an individual's or group's perception of a number of environmental factors relevant to satisfaction of their needs and the resulting choice of location. The information needed to build a truly adequate and realistic model is perhaps unknowable. Even if the information were available, it would increase model complexity to the extent that a computer could not handle the simulation at reasonable expense.

In a sense, however, these weaknesses can be viewed as strengths: a pattern of settlement similar to reality was generated with relatively little complexity. Reality was thus simplified. Also, on a more mundane level, the model is robust because of its general nature, and it could be applied to examination of settlement systems for other cultural manifestations of a similar level. Simplicity and generality also allow one to effectively follow the interaction of variables that influence location.

Simulation provides the key to comprehending locational behavior through this ability to follow the development of settlement patterns. One can more easily visualize the system at work because as model builder, one becomes almost personally involved with the culture, much like the ethnographer who becomes personally involved with "his" people while watching their development. The model is rather like a novel; a set of characters is created, a set of circumstances to which they must react is established, and the question is asked: How will they behave? Simulation allows one to find out, given the rules, if the reactions are as anticipated. This involvement promotes serendipity. One often encounters a totally unexpected situation that offers insight into the particular model's behavior or one's own thinking about the modelled processes themselves. With serendipity come new avenues of experimentation.

In terms of locational processes as modelled here, the computer printout is rather limiting. Involvement in the modelled processes could be greatly facilitated by equipment that provides a more instantaneous feedback to the model builder and provides visual output other than a computer printout.

Simulation provides a ready analysis of a model's weak areas and thereby suggests possible approaches for further research. For Glenwood I, the demographic data became a key weak point. More research needs to be done. If these data cannot be gathered from the Glenwood locality itself, they can perhaps be brought to the model by analogy from another Central Plains tradition locality. Sources for more adequate prehistoric environmental data must be gathered as well. For the Glenwood locality, this means greater attention to the recovery and analysis of natural environmental materials.

Even though the locational rules used in Glenwood I generated an adequate settlement distribution, the impact of other cultural phenomena on locational decisions remains a question. No attempt was made to consider contact with groups outside the locality other than in the acquisition of marriageable males. Contact with non-Central Plains tradition cultures was likewise not considered, nor was what happened to the Glenwood locality after 150 years. Micro-phenomena involved in settlement could be programmed into such a model with the attendant risk of complicating the model beyond understanding. These phenomena include house size, artifact distribution, and cultural "software" such as religious activities, none of which were considered in the present Glenwood I model. The resultant view of a near total system would be interesting, but would have obscured the central question of locational processes. In essence, a model like Glenwood I could be extended far beyond the limited form described here to an even more realistic level. System boundaries can be set arbitrarily, encompassing ever more variables, but with the ever-present risk of the complexity dilemma. That is, the model might become as complex as the data it was intended to explain, and therefore might be equally difficult to understand.

The Glenwood I simulation, because it is not overly specific to the Glenwood locality, could be applicable to most Central Plains tradition localities. Specific environmental data would need to be incorporated as would life table data if they existed. To this degree, Glenwood I may also be applied, with very limited modification, to other cultural traditions with similar social structure and at least a semi-sedentary settlement pattern. In this sense Glenwood I is robust.

Simulation is not a panacea for archaeological problems; it has many liabilities. Perhaps the most important liability is the complexity dilemma. In a sense the computer is very limiting. One can conceptualize many possibilities for a model that are beyond the capabilities of the language selected for model synthesis, or at least beyond one's programming abilities. This is most frustrating. Even when one has managed to program a particular idea, a set of parameters of initialization might foul the mechanisms on the tenth iteration. Logical errors easily creep into a complicated program and are difficult to detect and eliminate. Verification presented the single most time-consuming stage in the development of Glenwood I. Formal validation for archaeological problems is most often impossible; there is no modelled system left for experimentation. Consequently, all inferences must be questioned. Finally, and not least important, computer simulation is expensive. Computer time alone for this model cost nearly $3000. In part, this derives from the model's complexity and the model builder's lack of programming ability. Even with proper operation, each run of the simulation cost about $25.

In all, the benefits to be gained from total society simulations outweigh the liabilities. If one remembers that simulation proves nothing about prehistory, it can be a most useful tool. Simulation is simply a methodological device that allows the researcher a great deal of freedom to hypothesize and that provides limited tests of those hypotheses. For the archaeologist, simulation allows a shift away from the artifacts themselves toward their systemic context and their behavioral correlates. Simulation makes total society study in archaeology feasible; its implementation, as has been demonstrated here, is a logical methodological extension of the use of systems analysis in archaeology.

Summary

Two general problems have been considered here: how locational decisions are made, and what impact those decisions have on the development of prehistoric settlement patterns. Since these archaeological questions share roots with geography's study of locational behavior and spatial analysis, the development of settlement study in archaeology was outlined specifically in terms of overlapping geographic perspectives. Archaeology and geography were seen to share a concern with the impact of environment, both natural and social, on the locational decision making process. Since this concern is an old one in geography, but is a relatively recent development in archaeology, the suggestion was made that archaeology could directly borrow techniques commonly used by geographers, especially computer simulation. Theoretical viewpoints regarding locational behavior were also seen as useful to archaeology. Criticism of optimizing frameworks resulted in the opinion that satisficing models better mirrored real decision making processes.

From this background, a particular archaeological problem, the nature of settlement systems prevalent among Central Plains tradition peoples of the Glenwood locality of southwest Iowa, was analyzed. The simular model building procedure offered by Mihram (1972a) was used to develop a model to account for the settlement distribution known in the locality. A series of hypotheses made by Anderson and Zimmerman (n.d.) formed the core of the model's algorithm. The particular settlement system constructed was based on archaeological data from the locality and analogy to similar cultures. This system was synthesized into a computer program in the simulation language SIMSCRIPT. The model was then verified and calibrated to operate as planned. Seven runs of the simulation were completed and analyzed. The first run incorporated all the variables considered by Anderson and Zimmerman. Validation demonstrated that the original hypotheses would not have produced the known settlement pattern. Successive runs altered various model structures and parameters in order to test particular hypotheses. The run that produced the most realistic results suggested the following conclusions about the settlement system in the Glenwood locality:

1) Temporal duration was probably no longer than 150 years.
2) Climatic change, if it occurred, had little or no impact on settlement.
3) Population levels were low, rarely exceeding 100 persons.
4) Large clusters of lodges were extremely rare; if they occurred, they resulted either from reuse or the close location of sisters. Probably no cluster at any point in time had more than four inhabited lodges.

Finally, the efficacy of simulation modelling of locational processes was discussed from the viewpoint of having worked with the Glenwood I model. The weaknesses of such simular models are outweighed by the amount of involvement in the processes the investigator is allowed. Simulation was judged to be an extremely complex but most useful technique for the examination of human locational processes.

Appendix:
Glenwood I Program List

```
     SIMULATION
*
T WOMAN8
     T MOTHR 11/2 P
     T FDAUG 12/2 P
     T LDAUG 21/2 P
     T SDAUG 22/2 P
     T LODG  31/2 P
     T FCHIL 32/2 P
     T WBDTE 41/2 F
     T HBDTE 42/2 F
     T SRESI 51/2 P
     T WDIE  52/2 F
     T HDIE  61/2 F
     T LCHIL 62/2 P

     WOMAN IS THE MAIN ENTITY OF THE SYSTEM. THE ATTRIBUTES ARE

     MOTHR   POINTER TO THE MOTHER OF THIS WOMAN
     FDAUG   POINTERS FOR DAUGHTER SET OWNED BY THIS WOMAN
     LDAUG   POINTER FOR DAUGHTER SET THIS WOMAN IS A MEMBER OF
     SDAUG   POINTER FOR DAUGHTER SET THIS WOMAN IS A MEMBER OF
     LODG    POINTER TO THE LODGE ENTITY THIS WOMAN RESIDES IN
     SRESI   POINTER FOR SET OF RESIDENTS THIS WOMAN IS A MEMBER OF
     FCHIL   POINTER FOR THE CHILDREN SET OF THIS WOMAN
     WBDTE   TIME VARIABLE CONTAINING WOMANS DATE OF BIRTH
     HBDTE   SAME FOR HUSBAND
     WDIE    TIME VARIABLE CONTAINING DEATH DATE FOR THIS WOMAN
     HDIE    SAME FOR HER HUSBAND

T MATRH2
*
     MATRH IS AN ENTITY WITH THE FIRST TWO WORDS THE SAME AS THOSE IN
     THE ENTITY WOMAN. AFTER A WOMAN DIES IT IS USED TO HOLD THE INFORMATION
*    FOR THE MATRIARCHY UNTIL IT IS NO LONGER NEEDED
T LODGE4
     T SHAUS 11/2 P
     T FRESI 12/2 P
     T LOCX  21/4 I
     T LOCY  22/4 I
     T SIZE  24/4 I
     T DCONS 32/2 F
     T NTYP1 41/4 I
     T NTYP2 42/4 I
     T NTYP3 43/4 I
     T NTYP4 44/4 I
```

```
      T FARM    23/4  L
      T PHAUS   31/2  P
*
*  LODGE IS THE ENTITY WHICH NAMES THE INFORMATION CONCERNING THE LODGE
*     SHAUS    POINTER FOR THE SET OF HOUSES IN THE SYSTEM
*     FRESI    POINER FOR THE SET OF RESIDENTS OWNED BY THIS LODGE
      LOC X    THE X LOCATION OF THE HOUSE
      LOC Y    THE Y LOCATION OF THE HOUSE
      SIZE     SIZE OF HOUSE IN SQUARE FEET
      DCONS    TIME VARIABLE WHICH IS THE DATE OF CONSTRUCTION
      NTYP1
      NTYP2
      NTYP3
*     NTYP4    THE NUMBER OF UNITS OF EACH TYPE OWNED BY THIS LODGE
*     FARM     LOGICAL VARIABLE TRUE IF THE RESIDENTS FARM
*
   T CHILD4
      T SCHIL   11/2  P
      T SEX     12/2  I
      T BDATE   3     F
      T MARDT   4     F
      T DDATE   21/2  F
      T PCHIL   22/2  P
*
*  CHILD ENTITIES BELONG TO A WOMAN AND HOLD INFORMATION ABOUT EACH NMARRIED
*     CHILD
*     SCHIL    POINTER TO NEXT CHILD IN SET OF CHILDREN
*     SEX      INDICATES THE SX OF THE CHILD
*     BDATE    TIME VARIABLE-BIRTHDATE
*     MARDT    TIME VARIABLE-MARRIAGE DATE
*     DDATE    TIME VARIABLE-DEATH DATE
   N MARY 4
      N BMTHR   41/2  P
      N BRIDE   42/2  P
*
*  MARY IS AN EVENT WHICH OCCURS WHEN A FEMALE CHILD MARRYS.
*
*     BMTHR    THE WOMAN WHOSE CHILD IS TO MARRY
*     BRIDE    THE CHILD SCHEDULED TO MARRY.
*
   N DEATH4
      N DWOMN   4     P
*
*  DEATH IS AN EVENT SCHEDULED WHEN A WOMAN DIES
*
*     DWOMN    THE DYING WOMAN POINTER
*
```

295
296
300
305
310
315
320
325
330
335
340
345
350
355
360
365
370
375
380
385
390
395
400
405
410
415
420
425
430
435
440
445
450
455
460
465
470
475
480
485
490
495
500
505
510

```
 515   N SEASN4
 520  *** SEASON OCCURS PERIODICALLY TO DO SYSTEM MAINTENANCE
 525   N SNAP 4
 530  *** SNAP OCCURS PERIODICALLY TO PRINT OUT INFORMATION ABOUT THE SYSTEM
 535   N BIRTH4    N PREG    4    P
 540  *** BIRTH OCCURS WHEN A CHILD IS SCHEDULED TO APPEAR.
 545  *** PREG    POINTER TO THE EXPECTING WOMAN
 550
 555             1PHAUS 0    P
 560            35LHAUS 0    P
 565  *** A POINTER TO THE SET OF LODGES OWNED BY THE SYSTEM
 570
 575             2MMRTS 0    I
 580             3WMRTS 0    I
 585             4PARTS 0    I
 586             5MMARS 0    I
 590             6WMARS 0    I
 595
 600             7TMMRT 0    I
 605             8TWMRT 0    I
 610             9TPART 0    I
 615            10TMMAR 0    I
 620            11TWMAR 0    I
 625
 630
 635            12MMORT     F SL
 640            13WMORT     F SL
 645            14PARTB     F SL
 650            15MMARG     F SL
 655            16WMARG     F SL
 660
 665  *** THE ABOVE ARE SEVRAL RANDOM TABLES AND THEIR ASSOCIATED SUBSCRIPT
 670  *** CONTAINING VARIABLES.  THE BOTTOM ELEMENTS ARE THE TABLES, THE
 675  *** MIDDLE ELEMENTS ARE CORRESPONDING ACCESS VARIABLES, AND THE TOP
 680  *** ELEMENTS ARE THE NUMBER OF SUBSCRIPT HOLDING VARIABLES. THUS
 685  *** THERE ARE SEVERAL TABLES OF EACH TYPE ACCESIBLE BY SBSCRIPT.
 690  *** THE ACCESS WILL BE BY LINEAR INTERPOLATION.
 695
 700
 705
 710
 715
 720
 725   MMORT  MALE MORTALITY TABLE
 730
```

```
*     WMORT   WOMAN MORTALITY TABLE
*     PARTB   TABLE FOR FIRST PARTURITION
*     MMARG   MALE MARRIAGE TABLE
*     WMARG   FEMALE MARRIAGE TABLE
*
                17SMOTR 0    P
                18SNPIN 0    P
                19SSNIN 0    F
                20FEMSX 0    I
*
*     SMOTR   THE SYSTEM MOTHER OINTER VARIABLE
*     SNPIN   INTERVAL AT WHICH SNAP OCCURS
*     SSNIN   INTERVAL AT WHICH SEASN OCCURS
*     FEMSX   INDICATES WHICH VALUE OF SEX DENOTES WOMAN
*
                21LOCXD E
                22LOCYD E
                23CLODG 2   /2  P
                24TYPE  2   /4  I
                25ELEV  2   /2  I
*
*     LOCXD   ENTITY WHICH OWNS THE X COORDINATE OF THE REGION
*     LOCYD   ENTITY WHICH OWNS THE Y COORDINATE OF THE REGION
*     CLODG   POINTER TO THE LODGE WHICH INHABITS THE LAND UNIT NAMED
*     TYPE    TYPE OF LAND UNIT NAMED
*     ELEV    ELEVATION OF LAND UNIT NAMED
*
                26TYPE1 0    I
                27TYPE2 0    I
                28TYPE3 0    I
                29TYPE4 0    I
*
*     THESE ARE FOUR VARIABLES USED TO PAS INFORMATION AROUND
*     ABOUT HOW MUCH OF EACH LAND UNIT IS OWNED
*
                30SBRTE 0    I
                31BRATE 1    P
*
*     AN ARRAY AND SUBSCRIPT HOLDER WHICH CONTAINS INFORMATION FOR
*     SCHEDULING BIRTHS AFTER THE FIRST
*
                32CRDPR 0    I
                33CRDPC 0    I
                34LGLCA 2    I
```

735
740
745
750
755
760
765
770
775
780
785
790
795
800
805
810
815
820
825
830
835
840
845
850
855
860
865
870
875
880
885
890
895
900
905
910
915
920
925
930
935
940
945
950
955

```
*        CONTAINS X-Y INCREMENTS FOR INSPECTING POTENTIAL NEW LODGE            960
*        LOCATIONS AT THE EIGHT CARDINAL POINTS, USED BY CHECK                 965
*                                                         DAUG1 P              970
*        THE SET OF DAUGHTERS OWNED BY A WOMAN                                  975
*                                                         HAUS0  RDCONS L       980
*        THE SET OF ALL LODGES OWNED BY THE SYSTEM                              985
*                                                         CHIL1  RMARDT L       990
*        THE SET OF CHILDREN OWNED BY A WOMAN                                   995
.                                                         RESI1L                1000
*        THE SET OF RESIDENTS OWNED BY A LODGE                                  1005
                                                                  PAD  I        1010
                                                                               1015
         EVENTS                                                                 1020
         3 EXOGENOUS                                                            1025
              START(1)                                                          1030
              TRNS1(2)                                                          1035
              STOP(3)                                                           1040
         5 ENDOGENOUS                                                           1045
              SEASN                                                             1050
              MARY                                                              1055
              DEATH                                                             1060
              BIRTH                                                             1065
              SNAP                                                              1070
                                                                               1075
         END                                                                    1080
         EXOGENOUS EVENT START                                                  1085
         LOGICAL FAIL                                                           1090
         INTEGER SR,SC                                                          1095
         CALL TRACE(1)                                                          1100
                                                                               1105
*        SET UP THE MAP.                                                        1110
*                                                                              1115
         DO TO END, FOR I - (1) (400)                                           1120
X        READ(1,1)SR,SC,LR,(TYPE((SR-1)*10 LR,(SC-1)*10 J),                     1125
    &    ELEV((SR-1)*10 LR,(SC-1)*10 J),J_1,10)                                 1130
X 1      FORMAT(2I1,I2,10(I2,I5))                                               1135
         END LOOP                                                               1140
*        CREATE THE OWNER WOMAN NODE, SET UP POINTER TO IT                      1145
*                                                                              1150
         CREATE WOMAN CALLED MOM                                                1155
         LET SMOTR - MOM                                                        1160
*                                                                              1165
*        SET UP THE INITIAL HOUSEHOLDS                                          1170
*                                                                              1175
         READ NHOUS                                                             1180
         FORMAT(I5)
```

```
        DO TO LP1, FOR I = (1)  (NHOUS)
        CREATE WOMAN
        FILE WOMAN IN DAUG(MOM)
        CREATE LODGE
        FILE LODGE IN HAUS
        FILE WOMAN IN RESI(LODGE)
        LET DCONS(LODGE) = TIME
        LET LODG(WOMAN) = LODGE
        LET FARM(WOMAN) = .FALSE.
        LET MOTH(WOMAN) = MOM
*
*
*    GET ADDITIONAL INFORMATION ON THE WOMAN

        READ  WBDTE(WOMAN),HBDTE(WOMAN), LOCX(LODGE),LOCY(LODGE)
     &        NCH
        FORMAT(2D4.0,3I5)
        LET WDIE(WOMAN) = WBDTE(WOMAN)   WMORT(TWMRT)
        LET HDIE(WOMAN) = HBDTE(WOMAN)   MMORT(TMMRT)
        CREATE DEATH
        LET DWOMN(DEATH) = WOMAN
        CAUSE DEATH AT WDIE(WOMAN)
*
*
*    LETS HAVE SOME REPRODUCTION HERE.

BLP     LET NLT = 0
        LET BRTH = WBDTE(WOMAN)   PARTB(TPART)
        LET NLT = NLT + 1
        IF NLT GT 20, GO TO NCH
        IF BRTH LT TIME  .75, GO TO BLP
        IF BRTH GT WDIE(WOMAN), GO TO NCH
        CREATE BIRTH
        CAUSE BIRTH AT BRTH
        LET PREG(BIRTH) = WOMAN
*
*
*    SET UP CHILDREN OF WOMAN

NCH     IF NCH EQ 0, GO TO NOK
        DO TO CHLP, FOR J = (1) (NCH)
        CREATE CHILD
        FILE CHILD IN CHIL(WOMAN)
        READ  SEX(CHILD),BDATE(CHILD)
        FORMAT(I5,D4.0)
        IF SEX(CHILD) EQ FEMSX, GO TO FEM
        LET MARDT(CHILD) = BDATE(CHILD)   MMARG(TMMAR)
        LET DDATE(CHILD) = BDATE(CHILD)   MMORT(TMMRT)
```

```
1410   FEM    GO TO CHLP
1415          LET MARDT(CHILD) - BDATE(CHILD)    WMARG(TWMAR)
1420          LET DDATE(CHILD) - BDATE(CHILD)    WMORT(TWMRT)
1425   CHLP   LOOP
1430   *
1435   **     SET HOUSE SIZE AND CLAIM TERRITORY
1440   *
1445   NOK    CALL HSIZ(LODGE)
1450          CALL CLRTP
1455          CALL TRTYP(WOMAN)
1460          CALL TRADD(LODGE,*FAIL)
1465          CALL PWOMN(WOMAN)
1470          IF .NOT. FAIL,GO TO LP1
1475          WRITE ON 6
1480          FORMAT(*    FAILURE TO ADD TERRITORY IN START*)
1485   LP1    LOOP
1490          CREATE SNAP
1495          CAUSE SNAP AT TIME
1500          CREATE SEASN
1505          CAUSE SEASN AT TIME
1510          RETURN
1515          END
1520          EXOGENOUS EVENT TRNS1
1525   *
1530   ***    READ THE NEW MAX ELEVATION OF TYPE 1 ECO ZONES, AND RESET ANY
1535   ***    TOO HIGH TO TYPE 3.  READ NEW TABLE SUBSCRIPTS.
1540   *
1545          INTEGER NEL
1550          READ NEL,TMMRT,TWMRT,TPART,TMMAR,TWMAR
1555          FORMAT(6I5)
1560          DO TO 10,FOR I_(1)(NLOCXD)
1565          DO TO 10,FOR J_(1)(NLOCYD)
1570          IF ELEV(I,J) LE NEL,GO TO 10
1575          IF TYPE(I,J) NE 1,GO TO 10
1580          LET TYPE(I,J)   3
1585          IF CLODG(I,J) EQ POINTR(0),GO TO 10
1590          LET NTYP1(CLODG(I,J)) - NTYP1(CLODG(I,J)) -1
1595          LET NTYP3(CLODG(I,J)) - NTYP3(CLODG(I,J)) -1
1600   10     LOOP
1605          RETURN
1610          END
1615          EXOGENOUS EVENT STOP
1620          STOP
1625          END
1630          ENDOGENOUS EVENT SEASN
```

```
      POINTER LDG,FAM,KID
      LOGICAL FAIL
      DESTROY SEASN
      LET TIMEN - TIME  SSNIN
*
**    ACCESS ALL THE WOMAN NODES BY USING THE LODGES IN HAUS
**
      DO TO 10, FOR EACH LDG IN HAUS
      CALL CLRTP
REDO  DO TO 20, FOR EACH FAM IN RESI(LDG)
      CALL TRTYP(FAM)
20    LOOP
      IF NTYP1(LDG) LT TYPE1 OR NTYP2(LDG) LT TYPE2 OR
    & NTYP3(LDG) LT TYPE3 OR NTYP4(LDG) LT TYPE4, GO TO NEED
      GO TO OK
*
**    TERRITORY IS NEEDED.  IF CAN-T ADD TRY FARMING.  IF STILL NO GOOD
**    CHECK RELATIVES.
*
NEED  CALL TRADD(LDG,*FAIL)
      IF .NOT.FAIL, GO TO OK
      IF FARM(LDG), GO TO CHCK
      LET FARM(LDG) _ .TRUE.
      GO TO REDO
*
**    FOR NOW WE JUST KILL OFF (TO BE CHANGED)
**
CHCK  DO TO 30, FOR EACH FAM IN RESI(LDG)
      REMOVE FIRST CHILD FROM CHIL(FAM), IF NONE GO TO 30
      DESTROY CHILD
30    LOOP
*
**    IF HUSBAND DEAD, MARK HIM SO.
**
OK    DO TO 40,FOR EACH FAM IN RESI(LDG)
      IF HDIE(FAM) LT TIME,LET HDIE(FAM) _ 0
*
**    FIND CHILD WITH BIRTH OR DEATH SCHEDULED
**
      FIND FIRST CHILD OF FAMILY, FOR EACH KD IN CHIL(FAM),
    & WITH MARDT(KD) LE TIMEN OR DDATE(KD) LE TIMEN,
    & WHERE KID IS THE CHILD FOUND, IF NONE GO TO 40
      IF SEX (KID) EQ FEMSX, GO TO FEM
KILL  REMOVE KID FROM CHIL(FAM)
      DESTROY CHILD CALLED KID
```

```
1860  FEM      GO TO 40
1865           IF DDATE(KID) LE TIME, GO TO KILL
1870           CREATE MARY
1875           LET BMTHR(MARY) - FAM
1880           LET BRIDE(MARY) - KID
1885           CAUSE MARY AT MARDT(KID)
1890  40 LOOP
1895  10       LOOP
1900           CREATE SEASN
1905           CAUSE SEASN AT TIME   SSNIN
1910           RETURN
1915           END
1920           ENDOGENOUS EVENT MARY
1925           LOGICAL FAIL,B
1930           POINTER MOM,BRDE,FAM,LDG
1935  ***      RECOVER INFORMATION FROM EVENT NOTICE.
1940           LET MOM - BMTHR(MARY)
1945           LET BRDE - BRIDE(MARY)
1950           WRITE ON 6, TIME,INTEGR(MOM,INTEGR(BRDE)
1955           FORMAT(//,*MARRIAGE AT *,M4.2.2,* MOTHER *,O6
1960        &  ,* BRIDE *,O6)
1965           DESTROY MARY
1970  ***      CREATE THE NEW WOMAN NODE AND FILL IN.
1975           CREATE WOMAN
1980           LET MOTH(WOMAN) - MOM
1985           LET WBDTE(WOMAN) - BDATE(BRDE)
1990           LET HBDTE(WOMAN) - BDATE(BRDE) -3. - 6.*RANDM
1995           LET WDIE(WOMAN) - DDATE(BRDE)
2000  ***      MAKE SURE THE BRIDEGROOM IS NOT MORIBUND
2005  MLP      LET DMRT - HBDTE(WOMAN)   MMORT(TMMRT)
2010           IF DMRT LT TIME, GO TO MLP
2015           LET HDIE(WOMAN) - DMRT
2020           CREATE DEATH
2025           CAUSE DEATH AT WDIE(WOMAN)
2030           LET DWOMN(DEATH) - WOMAN
2035  ***      LETS KEEP IN MORAL NOW.
2040           LET NLT - 0
```

```
BLP  LET BRTH = WBDTE(WOMAN)    PARTB(TPART)           2085
     LET NLT = NLT + 1                                 2090
     IF NLT GT 20, GO TO NCH                           2095
     IF BRTH LT TIME - .75, GO TO BLP                  2100
     IF BRTH GT WDIE(WOMAN), GO TO NCH                 2105
     LET B = .TRUE.                                    2110
     CREATE BIRTH                                      2115
     CAUSE BIRTH AT BRTH                               2120
     LET PREG(BIRTH) = WOMAN                           2125
*                                                      2130
**   FIND OUT IF THIS IS THE LAST FEMALE CHILD. IF SO, TAKE OVER  2135
**   PARENT=S TERRITORY.  THERWISE LOCATE A NEW TERRITORY.        2140
*                                                      2145
NCH  REMOVE BRDE FROM CHIL(MOM), IF NONE GO TO ENOW    2150
     DESTROY CHILD CALLED BRDE                         2155
     FIND FIRST SISTER, FOR EACH SIB IN CHIL(MOM), WITH 2160
   & SEX(SIB) EQ FEMSX, IF NONE GO TO NOS              2165
     GO TO NEWT                                        2170
NOS  LET LODG(WOMAN) = LODG(MOM)                       2175
     FILE WOMAN IN RESI(LODG(MOM))                     2180
     FILE WOMAN IN DAUG(MOM)                           2185
*                                                      2190
**   FIND OUT IF THERE IS ENOUGH RESOURCE HERE.        2195
*                                                      2200
     CALL CLRTP                                        2205
     DO TO RES, FOR EACH FAM IN RESI(LODG(WOMAN))      2210
     CALL TRTYP(FAM)                                   2215
RES  LOOP                                              2220
     LET LDG = LODG(WOMAN)                             2225
     IF NTYP1(LDG) GE TYPE1 AND NTYP2(LDG) GE TYPE2 AND 2230
   & NTYP3(LDG) GE TYPE3 AND NTYP4(LDG) GE TYPE4, GO TO ENOW  2235
     CALL TRADD(LDG,*FAIL)                             2240
     IF FAIL,CALL MOVE(LDG)                            2245
ENOW WRITE ON 6                                        2250
     FORMAT(S10,*BRIDE STAYED IN PARENTS HOUSE*)       2255
     CALL PWOMN(WOMAN)                                 2260
     RETURN                                            2265
*                                                      2270
**   HERE WE NEED TO LOCATE A NEW TERRITORY.           2275
*                                                      2280
NEWT CREATE LODGE                                      2285
     LET FARM(LODGE) = .FALSE.                         2290
     FILE WOMAN IN RESI(LODGE)                         2295
     LET LODG(WOMAN) = LODGE                           2300
     LET LOCX(LODGE) = LOCX(LODG(MOM))                 2305
```

```
2310        LET LOCY(LODGE) = LOCY(LODG(MOM))
2315        LET DCONS(LODGE) = TIME
2320        CALL HSIZ(LODGE)
2325        CALL CLRTP
2330        CALL TRTYP(WOMAN)
2335        CALL MOVE(LODGE,*FAIL)
2340        IF FAIL,GO TO MIGR
2345        FILE LODGE IN HAUS
2350        FILE WOMAN IN DAUG(MOM)
2355        WRITE ON 6
2360        FORMAT(S10,*BRIDE MOVES*)
2365        CALL PWOMN(WOMAN)
2370        RETURN
2375 MIGR   CALL RELE(LODGE)
2380        CANCEL DEATH
2385        IF B, CANCEL BIRTH
2395        DESTROY WOMAN
2400        RETURN
2405        END
2410        ENDOGENOUS EVENT BIRTH
2415        POINTER PWMN
2420        LET PWMN = PREG(BIRTH)
2425        DESTROY BIRTH
2430        WRITE ON 6, TIME,INTGR(PWMN)
2435        FORMAT(//,*BIRTH AT *,M4.2.2,* MOTHER *,06)
2440
2445 * *
2450 *      SET UP THE CHILD ENTITY.
2455
2460        CREATE CHILD
2465        LET SEX(CHILD) = RANDI(0,1)
2470        LET BDATE(CHILD) = TIME
2475        IF SEX(CHILD) EQ FEMSX, GO TO FEM
2480        LET MARDT(CHILD) = MMARG(TMMAR)  TIME
2485        LET DDATE(CHILD) = MMORT(TMMRT)  TIME
2490        GO TO FILE
2495 FEM    LET MARDT(CHILD) = WMARG(TWMAR)  TIME
2500        LET DDATE(CHILD) = WMORT(TWMRT)  TIME
2505 FILE   FILE CHILD IN CHIL(PWMN)
2510        WRITE ON 6, INTGR(CHILD),SEX(CHILD),MARDT(CHILD),DDATE(CHILD)
2515        FORMAT(S20,*CHILD IS *,06,* SEX *,I1,* MARRIGE DATE *,M4.2.2,
2520      & * DEATH DATE *,M4.2.2)
2525 * *
2530 *      SCHEDULE NEXT BIRTH.
2535        LET N = TIME - WBDTE(PWMN)   3.
```

148

```
10      LET FACT _ 1.
        DO TO 10, FOR EACH KID IN CHIL(PWMN)
        LET FACT _ FACT * .9
        LOOP
        LET SUM _ 0.
        DO TO 20, FOR I _ (N) (SBRTE)
        LET SUM _ SUM _ FACT * BRATE(I)
        IF RANDM LT SUM, GO TO 25
20      LOOP
        RETURN
25      CREATE BIRTH
        CAUSE BIRTH AT WBDTE(PWMN)  FLOAT(I)
        LET PREG(BIRTH) _ PWMN
        RETURN
        END
*       ENDOGENOUS EVENT DEATH
*       POINTER WOMN,OLSIS
*
*       IF HUSBAND OR WIFE STILL LIVES, MARK HER DEAD AND END,
*       FOR THE FAMILY WILL CONTINUE UNDER THE SURVIVOR,
*
        LET WOMN _ DWOMN(DEATH)
        DESTROY DEATH
        WRITE ON 6,TIME,INTEGR(WOMN)
        FORMAT(//,*DEATH OCCURS AT TIME *,M4.2.2,* WOMAN IS *,.06)
        IF HDIE(WOMN) EQ 0 OR WDIE(WOMN) EQ 0, GO TO DOIT
        LET WDIE(WOMN) _ 0
        CREATE DEATH
        LET DWOMN(DEATH) _ WOMN
        CAUSE DEATH AT HDIE(WOMN)
        RETURN
*
*       FIND PLACE TO PUT CHILDREN.
*
DOIT    FIND MAGE _ MAX OF TIME - WBDTE(KID), FOR EACH KID IN
     &  DAUG(WOMN), WHERE OLSIS IS THE OLDEST DAUGHTER FOUND,
     &  IF NONE GO TO NOD
        GO TO MOV
NOD     FIND MAGE _ MAX OF TIME - WBDTE(SIS), FOR EACH SIS IN
     &  DAUG(MOTHR(WOMN)), WITH SIS NE WOMN, WHERE OLSIS IS THE
     &  OLDEST SISTER FOUND, IF NONE GO TO NONE
MOV     DO TO 10, FOR EACH KID IN CHIL(OLSIS)
10      FILE KID IN CHIL(WOMN)
        LOOP
        WRITE ON 6,INTEGR(OLSIS)
```

2540
2545
2550
2555
2560
2565
2570
2575
2580
2585
2590
2595
2600
2605
2610
2615
2620
2625
2630
2635
2640
2645
2650
2655
2660
2665
2670
2675
2680
2685
2690
2695
2700
2705
2710
2715
2720
2725
2730
2735
2740
2745
2750
2755
2760

```
            FORMAT($20,*MOVE ALL KIDS TO WOMAN *,O6)
            GO TO GOON
NONE        DO TO 11, FOR EACH KID IN CHIL(WOMN)
            REMOVE KID FROM CHIL (WOMN)
            DESTROY CHILD CALLED KID
11          LOOP
            WRITE ON 6
            FORMAT($20,*NO PLACE FOR KIDS, KILL ALL*)
*
**  HOUSE OWNERSHIP PASSES TO ANOTHER WOMAN RESIDENT OF LODGE.
*
GOON        REMOVE WOMN FROM RESI(LODG(WOMN))
            FIND FIRST OTHR OCCUPANT OF SAME LODGE, FOR EACH OTHR IN
  &         RESI(LODG(WOMN)), IF NONE GO TO RELE
            CALL CHNG(LODG(WOMN))
            CALL HSIZ(LODG(WOMN))
            LET DCONS(LODG(WOMN)) _ TIME
            LET LODG(OTHR) _ LODG(WOMN)
            GO TO POIN
RELE        CALL RELE(LODG(WOMN))
*
**  IF LAST GRAND DAUGHTER IS TO DIE, DESTROY GRANDMOTHER.
*
POIN        DO TO 30, FOR EACH D1 IN DAUG(MOTHR(MOTHR(WOMN)))
            DO TO 30, FOR EACH D2 IN DAUG(D1)
            IF WDIE(D2) NE 0, GO TO 40
30          LOOP
*
**  FOUND THAT CAN DESTROY THE GRANDMOTHER.
*
            LET GM _ MOTHR(MOTHR(WOMN))
35          REMOVE FIRST D1 FROM DAUG(GM), IF NONE GO TO DST
            FILE D1 IN DAUG(SMOTR)
            LET MOTHR(D1) _ POINTR(0)
DST         DESTROY MATRH CALLED GM
*
**  MAKE A SMALLER NODE FOR THE DEAD WOMAN, AMATRILINE HOLDER.
*
40          CREATE MATRH
            LET MOTHR(MATRH) _ MOTHR(WOMN)
            LET FDAUG(MATRH) _ FDAUG(WOMN)
            LET LDAUG(MATRH) _ LDAUG(WOMN)
            LET SDAUG(MATRH) _ SDAUG(WOMN)
            RETURN
            END
```

2765
2770
2775
2780
2785
2790
2795
2800
2805
2810
2815
2820
2825
2830
2835
2840
2845
2850
2855
2860
2865
2870
2875
2880
2885
2890
2895
2900
2905
2910
2915
2920
2925
2930
2935
2940
2945
2950
2955
2960
2965
2970
2975
2980
2985

```
2990        ENDOGENOUS EVENT SNAP
2995        DESTROY SNAP
3000        WRITE ON 6, TIME
3005        FORMAT(*1DISPLAY OF TERRITORY AT TIME*,M4.2.2)
3010   X    WRITE(6,6)
3015        DO TO 10, FOR J     (1)(NLOCYD)
3020        WRITE(6,5)(PAD(CLODG(I,J)),I_1,NLOCXD)
3025   X 5  FORMAT(1HI,80A1,1HI)
3030   10   LOOP
3035   X    WRITE(6,6)
3040   X6   FORMAT(1HI,8(10H--------I))
3045        CREATE SNAP
3050        CAUSE SNAP AT TIME    SNPIN
3055        RETURN
3060        END
3065        SUBROUTINE CLRTP
3070        LET TYPE1_0
3075        LET TYPE2_0
3080        LET TYPE3_0
3085        LET TYPE4_0
3090        RETURN
3095        END
3100        SUBROUTINE TRTYP(FAM)
3105        POINTER FAM
3110   *
3115   *    FAM IS A WOMAN NODE. ACCUMULATE INTO THE TYPE NODES THE
3120   *    AMOUNT OF RESOURCES OF EACH TYPE NEEDED.
3125   *
3130        LET NAD _ 1
3135        IF HDIE(FAM) GT TIME, LET NAD _ 2
3140        LET NAD _ NAD _ 1, FOR EACH KID IN CHIL(FAM),
3145   6      WITH TIME - BDATE(KID) GT 12.
3150        LET TYPE1 _ TYPE1  4*NAD
3155        LET TYPE2 _ TYPE2  5*NAD
3160        LET TYPE3 _ TYPE3  2*NAD
3165        LET TYPE4 _ TYPE4  4*NAD
3170        DO TO CHLP, FOR EACH KID IN CHIL(FAM),WITH TIME - BDATE(KID)
3175   6      LE 12.
3180        LET TYPE1 _ TYPE1   2
3185        LET TYPE2 _ TYPE2   2
3190        LET TYPE3 _ TYPE3   1
3195        LET TYPE4 _ TYPE4   2
3200   CHLP LOOP
3205        IF .NOT.FAM(LODG(FAM)), RETURN
3210        LET TYPE1 _ 0
```

```
        LET TYPE2 - 0                                                     3215
        LET TYPE3 - 0                                                     3220
        LET TYPE4 - TYPE4/4                                               3225
        RETURN                                                           3230
        END                                                             3235
        SUBROUTINE RELE (LDG)                                           3240
        POINTER LDG                                                     3245
*                                                                       3250
**  RELEASE ALL THE TERRITORY OWNED BY A LODGE TO THE SYSTEM.           3255
**                                                                      3260
        WRITE ON 6,TIME, LOCX(LDG),LOCY(LDG),NTYP1(LDG),NTYP2(LDG)      3265
      &        ,NTYP3(LDG),NTYP4(LDG)                                   3270
        FORMAT(//,*AT TIME *,H4.2.2,* ALL THE TERRITORY OF LODGE AT*,   3275
      &   2I5,* WAS ABANDONED TYPES WERE *,4I4)                         3280
        LET N_0                                                         3285
        LET NT_0                                                        3290
        LET NCL_ NTYP1(LDG) NTYP2(LDG) NTYP3(LDG) NTYP4(LDG)            3295
        LET NSW_1                                                       3300
BLP     LET NX _ LOCX(LDG) - N                                          3305
        IF NX LT 1, GO TO FRST                                          3310
XDR     DO TO 10, FOR NY _ (MAX0(LOCY(LDG)-N,1))                        3315
      &        (MIN0(LOCY(LDG) N,NLOCYD))                               3320
        IF CLODG(NX,NY) NE LDG, GO TO 10                                3325
        LET CLODG(NX,NY) _ POINTR(0)                                    3330
        LET NT - NT 1 - POINTR(0)                                       3335
10      LOOP                                                            3340
        GO TO (FRST,SCND),NSW                                           3345
FRST    LET NSW _ 2                                                     3350
        LET NX _ LOCX(LDG), N                                           3355
        IF NX GT NLOCXD, GO TO SCND                                     3360
        GO TO XDR                                                       3365
SCND    LET NSW _ 1                                                     3370
        LET NY _ LOCY(LDG) - N                                          3375
        IF NY LT 1, GO TO YFR                                           3380
YDR     DO TO 20, FOR NX _ (MAX0(LOCX(LDG) -N ,1))                      3385
      &        (MIN0(LOCX(LDG) N-1,NLOCXD))                             3390
        IF CLODG(NX,NY) NE LDG, GO TO 20                                3395
        LET CLODG(NX,NY) - POINTR(0)                                    3400
        LET NT - NT 1                                                   3405
20      LOOP                                                            3410
        GO TO (YFR,YSC),NSW                                             3415
YFR     LET NSW _ 2                                                     3420
        LET NX GT LOCY(LDG), N                                          3425
        IF NX GT NLOCYD, GO TO YSC                                      3430
        GO TO YDR                                                       3435
```

```
YSC    LET NSW _ 1
*
*      FIND OUT IF ALL TERRITORY IS TAKEN CARE OF.
*
       IF NT EQ NCL, GO TO HAUS
       IF NT GT NCL, GO TO ER1
       LET N _ N 1
       IF LOCX(LDG) -N LE 1 AND LOCX(LDG) N GE NLOCXD AND
     & LOCY(LDG)-N LE 1 AND LOCY(LDG) N GE NLOCYD,GO TO ER1
       GO TO BLP
*
*      RELEASE THE HOUSE.
*
HAUS   REMOVE LDG FROM HAUS
       WRITE ON 6,DCONS(LDG),SIZE(LDG)
       FORMAT(*THE LODGE WAS ABANDONED HERE*/*THE DATE OF CONSTRUCTION*,
     & M4.2,* THE SIZE *,I5)
       DESTROY LODGE CALLED LDG
       RETURN
*
*      ERROR MESSAGES.
*
ER1    WRITE ON 6,NT,NCL
       FORMAT(S10,*IN RELE THE NUMBER OF RELEASED UNITS *,I3,
     & * DOES NOT EQUAL THE NUMBER OF CLAIMED UNITS*,I4)
       RETURN
       END
       SUBROUTINE TRADD(LDG,FAIL)
       LOGICAL FAIL
       INTEGER X,Y,ND(5),HV(5)
*
*      ADD NEW TERRITORY AS NEEDED.
*
       WRITE ON 6,INTEGR(LDG)
       FORMAT(S20,*ADDING TERRITORY FOR LODGE *,O6)
       LET FAIL _ .FALSE.
       LET X _ LOCX(LDG)
       LET Y _ LOCY(LDG)
*
*      RECORD HOW MUCH WE NEED AND HAVE OF EACH TYPE UNIT.
*
       LET ND(1) _ TYPE1
       LET ND(2) _ TYPE2
       LET ND(3) _ TYPE3
       LET ND(4) _ TYPE4
```

```
3440
3445
3450
3455
3460
3465
3470
3475
3480
3485
3490
3495
3500
3505
3510
3515
3520
3525
3530
3535
3540
3545
3550
3555
3560
3565
3570
3575
3580
3585
3590
3595
3600
3605
3610
3615
3620
3625
3630
3635
3640
3645
3650
3655
3660
```

153

```
        LET HV(1)   - NTYP1(LDG)
        LET HV(2)   - NTYP2(LDG)
        LET HV(3)   - NTYP3(LDG)
        LET HV(4)   - NTYP4(LDG)
**
**   NOW GATHER UP TERRITORY, UNTIL HAVE ENOUGH.
        LET N   0
        LET NSW   1
BLP     LET NX   X-N
        IF NX LT 1, GO TO XFR
XDR     DO TO 20, FOR NY   (MAX0(Y-N,1))(MIN0(Y N,NLOCYD))
        IF CLODG(NX,NY) NE  POINTR(0), GO TO 20
        IF ND(TYPE(NX,NY)) LE HV(TYPE(NX,NY)), GO TO 20
        LET CLODG(NX,NY)   LDG
        LET HV(TYPE(NX,NY)) - HV(TYPE(NX,NY)) 1
20      LOOP
        GO TO (XFR,XSC),NSW
XFR     LET NSW   2
        LET NX   X N
        IF NX GT NLOCXD, GO TO XSC
        GO TO XDR
XSC     LET NSW   1
        LET NY   Y-N
        IF NY LT 1, GO TO YFR
YDR     DO TO 30, FOR NX   (MAX0(X-N,1))(MIN0(X N-1,NLOCXD))
        IF CLODG(NX,NY) NE  POINTR(0), GO TO 30
        IF ND(TYPE(NX,NY)) LE HV(TYPE(NX,NY)), GO TO 30
        LET CLODG(NX,NY)   LDG
        LET HV(TYPE(NX,NY)) - HV(TYPE(NX,NY)) 1
30      LOOP
        GO TO (YFR,YSC),NSW
YFR     LET NSW   2
        LET NY   Y N
        IF NY GT NLOCYD, GO TO YSC
        GO TO YDR
YSC     LET NSW   1
**
**   FIND OUT IF ALL NEEDED TERRITORIES ARE CLAIMED.
        DO TO 40, FOR I   (1)(4)
        IF ND(I) GT HV(I), GO TO MORE
40      LOOP
        GO TO ENOF
MORE    LET N N 1
```

```
         IF X-N LT 1 OR X N GT NLOCXD OR Y-N LT 1 OR Y N GT NLOCYD        3890
       & ,GO TO ER2                                                       3895
CHM     IF N GT 25, GO TO FAIL                                            3900
        GO TO BLP                                                         3905
*                                                                         3910
*       ENOUGH TERRITORY IS FOUND.                                        3915
*                                                                         3920
ENOF    LET NTYP1(LDG) - HV(1)                                            3925
        LET NTYP2(LDG) - HV(2)                                            3930
        LET NTYP3(LDG) - HV(3)                                            3935
        LET NTYP4(LDG) - HV(4)                                            3940
        RETURN                                                            3945
*                                                                         3950
*       ERROR MESSAGES.                                                   3955
*                                                                         3960
ER2     WRITE ON 6                                                        3965
        FORMAT(*IN TRADD, EXPANDED TO MAP BOUNDARY.*)                     3970
        GO TO CHM                                                         3975
FAIL    WRITE ON 6                                                        3980
        FORMAT(*IN TRADD, EXPANDED MORE THAN 2.5 MILES OUT AND FAILED*)   3985
        LET FAIL - .TRUE.                                                 3990
        WRITE ON 6,ND(1),ND(2),ND(3),ND(4),HV(1),HV(2),HV(3),HV(4)       3995
        FORMAT(*NEED*,4I4,/,*HAVE*,4I4)                                   4000
        GO TO ENOF                                                        4005
        END                                                              4010
        SUBROUTINE MOVE(LDG,FL)                                           4015
        LOGICAL FAIL,FL                                                   4020
        POINTER LDG                                                       4025
        LET FL - .FALSE.                                                  4026
        WRITE ON 6, INTEGR(LDG)                                           4030
        FORMAT(S20,*MOVING LODGE *,O6)                                    4035
*                                                                         4040
*       MOVE A GROUP (I.E. THEIR LODGE) TO A NEW PLACE. CALL              4045
*       LGLOC WITH LODGE AND HAVE X,Y POSN OF LODGE CHANGED.              4050
*                                                                         4055
        CALL LGLOC(LDG)                                                   4060
*                                                                         4065
*       ADD TERRITORY.                                                    4070
*                                                                         4075
        CALL TRADD(LDG,*FAIL)                                             4080
        IF FAIL, GO TO ER1                                                4085
        RETURN                                                            4090
ER1     WRITE ON 6                                                        4095
        FORMAT(*IN MOVE, NOT ENOUGH TERRITORY WAS FOUND.*)                4100
        LET FL - .TRUE.                                                   4105
```

```
4110          RETURN
4115          END
4120          SUBROUTINE LGLOC(LDG)
4125          POINTER LDG
4130          INTEGER X,Y
4135   *
4140   *   GIVEN CURRENT X-Y POSITION OF LDG, MOVE IT TO ANEW PLACE.
4145   *   LOOK 1/2 MILE AWAY IN 8 CARDINAL POINTS, TAKE BEST PLACE.
4150   *
4155          LET RATIO _  0.
4160          LET X _ LOCX(LDG)
4165          LET Y _ LOCY(LDG)
4170          WRITE ON 6,INTEGR(LDG),X,Y
4175          FORMAT(S30,*FINDING A NEW LOC FOR LODGE *,06,* CURRENT POSN*,2I4)
4180          DO TO 10, FOR I _  (1) (8)
4181          IF TIME GT 825., CALL SNP
4185          CALL CHECK(X LGLCA(I,1),Y LGLCA(I,2),*R)
4190          IF R LT RATIO, GO TO 10
4195          LET NX _ X  LGLCA(I,1)
4200          LET NY _ Y  LGLCA(I,2)
4205          LET RATIO _ R
4210   10     LOOP
4215   *
4220   *   NOW FIND THE HIGHEST POINT IN THE NEW TERRITORY.
4225   *
4230          WRITE ON 6,NX,NY
4235          FORMAT(S35,*CENTER OF NEW TERRITORY*,2I4)
4240          LET MX _ 0
4245          DO TO 20, FOR I _  (NX-3) (NX 3)
4250          DO TO 20, FOR J _  (NY-3) (NY 3)
4255          IF MX GT ELEV(I,J),GO TO 20
4260          LET MX _ ELEV (I,J)
4265          LET NXF _ I
4270          LET NYF _ J
4275   20     LOOP
4280          LET LOCX(LDG) _ NXF
4285          LET LOCY(LDG) _ NYF
4290   *
4295   *   PRINT A MESSAGE.
4300   *
4305          WRITE ON 6, TIME, NXF,NYF
4310          FORMAT(//*AT TIME *,N4.2,2,*A NEW LODGE SITE WAS FOUND*,
4315        6  /*THE LOCATION WAS *,2I5)
4320          RETURN
4325          END
```

```
      SUBROUTINE CHECK(X,Y,R)
      INTEGER X,Y
      REAL NT(5),N
*
*     FIND THE ACCEPTABILITY RATIO OF THE REGION AROUND X-Y.
*
      DO TO 10, FOR I - (1) (4)
      LET NT(I) - 0
10    LOOP
      LET N   0
      DO TO 20, FOR I - (MAXO (X-3,1)) (MINO (X 3,NLOCXD))
      DO TO 20, FOR J - (MAXO (Y-3,1)) (MINO (Y 3,NLOCYD))
      IF CLODG(I,J) NE POINTR(0), GO TO 20
      LET NT(TYPE(I,J)) - NT(TYPE(I,J))   1.
      LET N - N   1.
20    LOOP
      IF N GT 25, GO TO OK
      LET R - 0.
      RETURN
OK    LET R   1. - ABS(4./15.-NT(1)/N) - ABS(1./3.-NT(2)/N)
    & - ABS(2./15.-NT(3)/N) - ABS(4./15.-NT(4)/N)
      WRITE ON 6,X,Y,R
      FORMAT(S40,*CHECKING LOCATION*,2I4,* RATIO IS *,D1.3)
      RETURN
      END
      SUBROUTINE CHANG(LDG)
      POINTER LDG
*
*     FIND JIGHEST NEW PLACE CLOSE BY.
*
      WRITE ON 6,TIME,LOCX(LDG),LOCY(LDG),DCONS(LDG),SIZE(LDG)
      FORMAT(//*AT TIME *,M4.2,* A LODGE AT *,2I5,* WAS ABANDONED*
    & /*THE DATE OF CONSTRUCTION WAS *,M4.2.2/
    & * THE SIZE WAS *,I5)
      LET MX   0
      DO TO 10, FOR I - (MAXO (LOCX(LDG)-2,1)
    &         (MINO (LOCX(LDG) 2,NLOCXD))
      DO TO 10, FOR J - (MAXO (LOCY(LDG)-2,1)
    &         (MINO (LOCY(LDG) 2,NLOCYD))
      IF I EQ LOCX(LDG) AND J EQ LOCY(LDG), GO TO 10
      IF MX GT ELEV(I,J), GO TO 10
      LET MX - ELEV(I,J)
      LET IS - I
      LET JS - J
10    LOOP
```

```
      LET LOCX(LDG) - IS
      LET LOCY(LDG) - JS
      WRITE ON 6, IS,JS
      FORMAT(/*A NEW HOUSE WAS ESTABLISHED AT *,2I5)
      RETURN
      END
      SUBROUTINE PWOMN(W)
      POINTER L
*
*     WRITE OUT INFORMATION ON WOMAN NODE.
*
      WRITE ON 6,INTEGR(W), INTEGR(MOTHR(W)),INTEGR(LODG(W)),WBDTE(W),
     & WDIE(W),WBDTE(W),HDIE(W)
      FORMAT(/*WOMAN NODE*,O6,/,S10,*MOTHER *,O6,* LODGE *,O6,/
     & S10,*WOMAN DATES*,2M6.2.2,* MAN DATES*,2M6.2.2)
      LET L - LODG(W)
      WRITE ON 6,LOCX(L),LOCY(L),SIZE(L),DCONS(L),NTYP1(L),NTYP2(L),
     & NTYP3(L),NTYP4(L),FARM(L),ELEV(LOCX(L),LOCY(L))
      FORMAT(/S15,*THE LODGE*/,S15,*LOCATION *,2I5,* SIZE *,I5,
     & * DATE OF CONSTRUCTION *,M4.2.2/S15,
     & * NUMBER OF UNITS OF EACH TYPE *,4I5,
     & * FARMING * L2,* ELEVATION *,I5//S20,*CHILDREN*)
      DO TO 10, FOR EACH K IN CHIL(W)
      WRITE ON 6,INTEGR(K),BDATE(K),MADT(K),DDATE(K),SEX(K)
      FORMAT(S25,O6,S2,*BORN *,M4.2.2,* MARY *,M4.2.2,* DIE *,
     & M4.2.2,* SEX *,I2)
10    LOOP
      RETURN
      END
      SUBROUTINE HSTI(L)
      POINTER L
*
***********
*    CHANGE THIS.
***********
*
      LET SIZE(L) - 80
      RETURN
      END
```

Bibliography

Abler, R., J. S. Adams, and P. Gould
1971　Spatial Organization: The Geographer's View of the World. Prentice-Hall, Inc., Englewood Cliffs, New Jersey.

Allen, W. L. and J. B. Richardson III
1971　The Reconstruction of Kinship from Archaeological Data: The Concepts, the Methods, and the Feasibility. American Antiquity, Vol. 36, No. 1, pp. 41-53.

Anderson, A. D.
1961　The Glenwood Local Sequence: A Local Sequence for a Series of Archaeological Manifestations in Mills County, Iowa. Journal of the Iowa Archeological Society, Vol. 10, No. 3.

Anderson, A. D. and B. Anderson
1960　Pottery Types of the Glenwood Foci. Journal of the Iowa Archeological Society, Vol. 9, No. 4, pp. 12-39.

Anderson, A. D. and L. J. Zimmerman
n.d.　Settlement-Subsistence Variability in the Glenwood Locality. (ms 1972).

Asch, N. B., R. I. Ford, and D. L. Asch
1972　Paleoethnobotany of the Koster Site: The Archaic Horizons. Illinois State Museum, Reports of Investigations 24. Illinois Valley Archaeological Program, Research Papers, Vol. 6. Springfield, Illinois.

Baerreis, D. A. and R. A. Bryson
1965　Climatic Episodes and the Dating of the Mississippian Cultures. Wisconsin Archeologist, Vol. 46, pp. 203-220.

1967　Climatic Change and the Mill Creek Culture of Iowa. Archives of Archaeology, No. 29. Madison, Wisconsin.

Beardsley, R. K. (Chairman)
1956　Functional and Evolutionary Implications of Community Patterning. In, Seminars in Archaeology: 1955, Memoirs of the Society for American Archaeology, 11, edited by Robert Wauchope, pp. 129-157.

159

Bell, E. H. and G. H. Gilmore
1936   The Newhawka and Table Rock Foci of the Nebraska Aspect. In, *Chapters in Nebraska Archaeology*, edited by Earl H. Bell, Vol. 1, No. 4, pp. 301-356. The University of Nebraska, Lincoln.

Berry, B. J. L.
1968   Approaches to Regional Analysis: A Synthesis. In, *Spatial Analysis: A Reader in Statistical Geography*, edited by B. J. L. Berry and D. F. Marble, pp. 24-34. Prentice-Hall, Inc., Englewood Cliffs, New Jersey.

Blumenstock, D. I. and C. W. Thornthwaite
1941   Climate and the World Pattern. In, Climate and Man, *1941 Yearbook of the United States Department of Agriculture*, edited by Gove Hambidge, pp. 1-64. Washington, D.C.

Bonini, C. P.
1963   *Simulation of Information and Decision Systems in the Firm.* Prentice-Hall, Inc., Englewood Cliffs, New Jersey.

Bowles, J. B.
1972   Distribution and Biogeography of Mammals of Iowa. MS, Ph.D. Dissertation, The University of Kansas, Lawrence.

Brennan, R. D.
1968   Simulation is Wha-a-at? Pt. II. In, *Simulation*, edited by John McLeod, pp. 5-12. McGraw Hill Book Company, New York.

Brockington, P.
1976   Archaeology As Anthropology: Reconstruction of Residence and Descent Patterns. *The Kansas Working Papers in Anthropology and Linguistics*, pp. 143-161. The University of Kansas, Lawrence.

Brown, L.
1968   Diffusion Dynamics: A Review and Revision of the Quantitative Theory of the Spatial Diffusion of Innovation. *Lund Studies in Geography, Series B, Human Geography*, No. 29. Lund, Sweden.

Brown, L. A.
1967   Pony Creek Archeology. *Publications in Salvage Archeology*, No. 5. Smithsonian Institution, River Basin Surveys, Lincoln.

Bryson, R. A.
1966   Air Masses, Streamlines, and the Boreal Forest. *Geographical Bulletin*, Vol. 8, pp. 228-269.

161

Bryson, R. A., D. A. Baerreis, and W. M. Wendland
1970   The Character of Late-Glacial and Post-Glacial Climatic Changes. In, Pleistocene and Recent Environments of the Central Great Plains, *Special Publication 3, Department of Geology, University of Kansas,* edited by Wakefield Dort and J. Knox Jones, pp. 53-74. Lawrence.

Bryson, R. A. and W. M. Wendland
1967   Tentative Climatic Patterns for Some Late Glacial and Post-Glacial Episodes in Central North America. In, Life, Land and Water, *Occasional Papers of the Department of Anthropology, University of Manitoba,* edited by W. J. Mayer-Oakes, pp. 271-298. Winnipeg, Canada.

Butzer, K. W.
1971   *Environment and Archeology: An Ecological Approach to Prehistory.* Aldine-Atherton, Chicago.

1973   Review of Climatic Change and the Mill Creek Culture of Iowa, Pts. I and II, *Journal of the Iowa Archeological Society,* Vol. 15 and 16. *Plains Anthropologist,* Vol. 18, No. 61, pp. 253-255.

Casteel, R. W.
1972   Two Static Maximum Population-Density Models for Hunter-Gatherers: A First Approximation. *World Archaeology,* Vol. 3, No. 3, pp. 19-40. London.

Chang, K. C.
1958   Study of Neolithic Social Groupings: Examples from the New World. *American Anthropologist,* Vol. 60, pp. 298-334.

1967   *Rethinking Archaeology.* Random House, New York.

1968   Toward a Science of Prehistoric Society. In, *Settlement Archaeology,* edited by K. C. Chang, pp. 1-9. National Press Books, Palo Alto, California.

1972   Settlement Patterns in Archaeology. *Addison-Modular Publication 24.* Addison-Wesley Publishing Company, Reading, Massachusetts.

Childe, V. G.
1925   *The Dawn of Western Civilization.* Alfred A. Knopf, New York.

1935   *Man Makes Himself.* Watts and Company, London.

162

1946   *What Happened in History.* Pelican Books, New York.

1956   *A Short Introduction to Archaeology.* Collier, New York.

1958   *The Dawn of European Civilization.* Alfred A. Knopf, New York.

Churchman, C. W., R. L. Ackoff, and E. L. Arnoff
1957   *Introduction to Operations Research.* John Wiley and Sons, Inc.,
        New York.

Clark, J. G. D.
1952   *Prehistoric Europe: The Economic Basis.* Stanford University Press,
        Stanford (1968).

1968   *Archaeology and Society.* Barnes and Noble, New York.

Clarke, D. L.
1968   *Analytical Archaeology.* Methuen and Company, Ltd., London.

1972   Models and Paradigms in Contemporary Archaeology. In,
        Models in Archaeology, edited by David L. Clarke, pp. 1-60.
        Methuen and Company, Ltd., London.

Cook, S. F. and R. F. Heizer
1968   Relationships Among Houses, Settlement Areas, and
        Population in Aboriginal California. In, *Settlement Archaeology,*
        edited by K. C. Chang, pp. 79-116. National Press Books, Palo
        Alto, California.

Cooper, Paul L.
1936   Archaeology of Certain Sites in Cedar County, Nebraska. In,
        Chapters in Nebraska Archaeology, Vol. 1, No. 1.

1939   Report of Explorations (1938). *Nebraska History Magazine,* Vol.
        20, No. 2, pp. 95-151.

Cutler, H. C. and L. W. Blake
1973   *Plants from Archeological Sites East of the Rockies.* Missouri
        Botanical Gardens, St. Louis.

Daniel, G.
1967   *The Origins and Growth of Archaeology.* Penguin Books,
        Baltimore.

1968   One Hundred Years of Old World Archaeology. In, *One
        Hundred Years of Anthropology,* edited by J. O. Brew, pp. 54-93.
        Harvard University Press, Cambridge.

Davenport, W.
1960   Jamaican Fishing: A Game Theory Analysis. *Yale University Publications in Anthropology*, No. 59. New Haven.

Davis, D. D. and P. R. Rowe
1960   Further Notes on the Glenwood Culture: The Stille Site. *Journal of the Iowa Archeological Society*, Vol. 9, No. 3, pp. 13-17.

Dean, S.
1881   Antiquities of Mills Co., Iowa. *Annual Report of the Smithsonian Institution for 1879*, pp. 528-532. Washington, D.C.

Deetz, J. F.
1965   The Dynamics of Stylistic Change in Arikara Ceramics. *Illinois Studies in Anthropology 4*. University of Illinois Press, Urbana.

Doran, J.
1970   Systems Theory, Computer Simulations, and Archaeology. *World Archaeology*, Vol. 1, No. 3, pp. 289-298.

Dutton, J. M. and W. H. Starbuck
1971   The Plan of the Book. In, *Computer Simulation of Human Behavior*, edited by John Dutton and William Starbuck, pp. 3-8. John Wiley and Sons, Inc., New York.

Dutton, J. M. and W. Briggs
1971   Simulation Model Construction. In, *Computer Simulation of Human Behavior*, edited by John Dutton and William Starbuck, pp. 103-126. John Wiley and Sons, Inc., New York.

Dyke, B. and J. W. MacCluer (Editors)
1974   *Computer Simulation in Human Population Studies.* Academic Press, New York.

Efron, B.
1971   Does an Observed Sequence of Numbers Follow a Simple Rule? *Journal of the American Statistical Association*, Vol. 66, pp. 552-559.

Eggan, F. (Editor)
1966   *The American Indian: Perspectives for the Study of Social Change.* Aldine Press, Chicago.

Eshelman, R. E.
n.d.   Faunal Analysis of the Lincoln I Site, 13 ML 119. (ms 1971).

164

Fennemen, N. E.
1938   *Physiography of Eastern United States.* McGraw Hill Book Company, New York.

Fischer, J. L.
1958   The Classification of Residence in Censuses. *American Anthropologist,* Vol. 60, pp. 508-517.

Fitch, J. M. and D. P. Branch
1960   Primitive Architecture and Climate. *Scientific American,* Vol. 23, No. 6, pp. 134-144.

Fox, Robin
1967   *Kinship and Marriage: An Anthropological Perspective.* Pelican Books, Baltimore.

Gilbert, J. P. and E. A. Hammel
1966   Computer Simulation and Analysis of Problems in Kinship and Social Structure. *American Anthropologist,* Vol. 68, No. 1, pp. 71-93.

Gilder, R. F.
1911   Discoveries Indicating an Unexploited Culture in Eastern Nebraska. *Records of the Past,* Vol. 10, Pt. 5, pp. 249-259. Washington, D.C.

1913   A Prehistoric "Cannibal" House in Nebraska. *Records of the Past,* Vol. 7, Pt. 3, pp. 107-116. Washington, D.C.

Goodenough, W. H.
1956   Residence Rules. *Southwestern Journal of Anthropology,* Vol. 12, pp. 22-37.

Gould, P. R.
1963   Man Against His Environment: A Game Theoretic Framework. *Annals of the Association of American Geographers.* Vol. 53, pp. 290-297.

Gradwohl, D. M.
1969   Prehistoric Villages in Eastern Nebraska. *Publications in Anthropology 4.* Nebraska State Historical Society, Lincoln.

Green, E. L.
1973   Locational Analysis of Prehistoric Maya Sites in Northern British Honduras. *American Antiquity,* Vol. 38, No. 3, pp. 279-293.

Gumerman, G. J. (Editor)
1971   The Distribution of Prehistoric Population Aggregates. *Prescott College Anthropological Reports 1.* Prescott, Arizona.

Hagerstrand, T.
1952   The Propagation of Innovation Waves. *Lund Studies in Geography, Series B, Human Geography,* No. 4. Lund, Sweden.

1957   Migration and Area. In, Migration in Sweden, *Lund Studies in Geography, Series B, Human Geography,* No. 13, edited by C. D. Hannerberg, Torsten Hagerstrand and S. V. Odeving. Lund, Sweden.

1967   *Innovation Diffusion as a Spatial Process.* University of Chicago Press, Chicago.

Haggett, P.
1965   *Locational Analysis in Human Geography.* Edward Arnold, Ltd., London.

Haggett, P. and R. J. Chorley
1967   *Models in Geography.* Methuen and Company, Ltd., London.

Harris, M.
1968   *The Rise of Anthropological Theory.* Thomas Y. Crowell Company, New York.

Hartshorne, R.
1958   The Concept of Geography as a Science of Space: From Kant and Humboldt to Hettner. *Annals of the Association of American Geographers,* Vol. 48, pp. 97-108.

Harvey, D.
1969   *Explanation in Geography.* Edward Arnold, Ltd., London.

Hays, D.
1965   Simulation: An Introduction for Anthropologists. In, *The Use of Computers in Anthropology,* edited by Dell Hymes, pp. 401-426. Mouton and Company, London.

Heider, K. G.
1967   Archaeological Assumptions and Ethnographical Facts: A Cautionary Tale from New Guinea. *Southwestern Journal of Anthropology,* Vol. 23, pp. 52-54.

Henning, D. R. (Editor)
1968   Climate Change and the Mill Creek Culture of Iowa, Pt. I. *Journal of the Iowa Archeological Society,* Vol. 15.

166

1969   Climate Change and the Mill Creek Culture of Iowa, Pt. II.
        Journal of the Iowa Archeological Society, Vol. 16.

Hettner, A.
1907   *Grundzuge der Landerkunde. Vol. 1, Europa.* Leipzig: Teubner.

Hill, A. T. and P. L. Cooper
1936   The Schrader Site; The Champe Site; Fremont 1. *Nebraska
        History Magazine*, Vol. 17, No. 4.

Hill, J. N.
1966   A Prehistoric Community in Eastern Arizona. *Southwestern
        Journal of Anthropology*, Vol. 22, pp. 9-30.

Hole, F. and R. Heizer
1965   *An Introduction to Prehistoric Archaeology.* Holt, Rinehart and
        Winston, New York.

1973   *An Introduction to Prehistoric Archaeology.* 3rd edition. Holt,
        Rinehart and Winston, New York.

Honeywell Information Systems, Inc.
1972   *SIMSCRIPT Reference Manual, Series 600/6000.* Honeywell
        Information Systems, Inc., Wellesley Hills, Massachusetts.

Ives, J. C.
1955   Glenwood Ceramics. *Journal of the Iowa Archeological Society*,
        Vol. 4, Nos. 3 and 4, pp. 2-32.

James, P. E.
1972   *All Possible Worlds: A History of Geographical Ideas.* The Odyssey
        Press. Indianapolis.

Johnson, P. C.
1972   Mammalian Remains Associated with Nebraska Phase
        Earthlodges in Mills County, Iowa. MS, Master's Thesis, The
        University of Iowa, Iowa City.

Jones, J. K., Jr.
1964   Distribution and Taxonomy of Mammals of Nebraska. *Museum
        of Natural History Publication 16.* The University of Kansas,
        Lawrence.

Judge, J. W.
1971   An Interpretative Framework for Understanding Site
        Locations. In, The Distribution of Prehistoric Population
        Aggregates, edited by George Gumerman, *Prescott College
        Anthropological Papers 1*, pp. 38-44. Prescott, Arizona.

Keyes, C. R.
1949   Four Iowa Archaeologies with Plains Affiliations. *Proceedings of the Fifth Plains Conference for Archaeology, Note Book No. 1,* pp. 96-97. Lincoln.

1951   Prehistoric Indians of Iowa. *Palimpsest,* Vol. 32, No. 8.

Krause, R. A.
1969   Correlation of Phases in Central Plains Prehistory. In, Two House Sites in the Central Plains: An Experiment in Archaeology, edited by W. Raymond Wood, *Plains Anthropologist Memoir 6,* Vol. 14, No. 44, Pt. 2, pp. 82-96.

1970   Aspects of Adaptation Among Upper Republican Subsistence Cultivators. In, Pleistocene and Recent Environments of the Central Great Plains, *Special Publication 3, Department of Geology, University of Kansas,* edited by Wakefield Dort and J. Knox Jones, pp. 103-116. Lawrence.

Lehmer, D. J.
1954   Archaeological Investigations in the Oahe Dam Area, South Dakota, 1950-51. *Bureau of American Ethnology, Bulletin 158. River Basin Surveys Papers,* No. 7. Washington, D.C.

1971   Introduction to Middle Missouri Archeology. *National Park Service, U.S. Department of the Interior, Anthropological Papers, 1.* Washington, D.C.

Longacre, W. A.
1964   Archaeology As Anthropology: A Case Study. *Science,* Vol. 144, pp. 1454-1455.

1966   Changing Patterns of Social Integration: A Prehistoric Example from the American Southwest. *American Anthropologist,* Vol. 68, pp. 94-102.

1968   Some Aspects of Prehistoric Society in East Central Arizona. In, *New Perspectives in Archeology,* edited by Lewis Binford and Sally Binford, pp. 89-102. Aldine, Chicago.

Lowenthal, D. (Editor)
1967   Environmental Perception and Behavior. *University of Chicago Department of Geography, Research Paper,* No. 109. Chicago.

Lowie, R.
1937   *The History of Ethnological Theory.* Holt, Rinehart and Winston, New York.

168

Marcus, J.
1973   Territorial Organization of the Classic Lowland Maya. *Science*, Vol. 180, pp. 911-916.

McLeod, J.
1968   Simulation is Wha-a-at? Cause for Confusion. In, *Simulation*, edited by John McLeod, pp. 1-4. McGraw Hill Book Company, New York.

Mihram, G. A.
1972a   The Modeling Process. *IEEE Transactions on Systems, Man, Cybernetics*, Vol. SMC-2, No. 5, pp. 621-629. Philadelphia.

1972b   Some Practical Aspects of the Verification and Validation of Simulation Models. *Operational Research Quarterly*, Vol. 23, pp. 17-19.

Mindeleff, C.
1900   Localization of Tusayan Clans. *Nineteenth Annual Report of the Bureau of American Ethnology*, Pt. 2, pp. 635-653. Washington, D.C.

Morgan, L. H.
1881   Houses and House-Life of the American Aborigines. *Contributions to North American Ethnology*, Vol. IV. Washington, D.C.

Morrill, R. L.
1965   Migration and the Spread and Growth of Urban Settlement. *Lund Studies in Geography, Series B, Human Geography*, No. 26. Lund, Sweden.

Mosimann, J. E. and P. S. Martin
1975   Simulating Overkill by Paleoindians. *American Scientist*, Vol. 63, pp. 304-313.

Murdock, G. P.
1949   *Social Structure*. The Macmillan Company, New York.

Naroll, R.
1962   Floor Area and Settlement Population. *American Antiquity*, Vol. 27, No. 4, pp. 587-589.

Odum, E. P.
1971   *Fundamentals of Ecology*. W. B. Saunders Company, Philadelphia.

Orr, E.
1963   Iowa Archaeological Reports 1934-1939. *Archives of Archaeology*, No. 20. University of Wisconsin Press, Madison.

Perry, W. J.
1924   *The Growth of Civilization*. London.

Peterson, N. F.
1923   *Flora of Nebraska*. State Printing Company, Lincoln, Nebraska.

Piggott, S.
1965   *Ancient Europe from the Beginnings of Agriculture to Classical Antiquity*. Aldine Publishing Company, Chicago.

Plog, F.
1968   Archeological Surveys. A New Perspective. MS, Master's Thesis, University of Chicago, Chicago.

Pred, A.
1967   Behavior and Location: Foundations for a Geographic and Dynamic Location Theory, Part I. *Lund Studies in Geography*, Series B, Human Geography, No. 27. Lund, Sweden.

1969   Behavior and Location: Foundations for a Geographic and Dynamic Location Theory, Part II. *Lund Studies in Geography*, Series B, Human Geography, No. 28. Lund, Sweden.

Proudfit, S. V.
1881   Antiquities of the Missouri Bluffs. *American Antiquarian*, Vol. 3, No. 4.

Pool, I. S.
1967   Computer Simulations of Total Societies. In, *The Study of Total Societies*, edited by E. Klausner, pp. 45-65. Doubleday and Company, Inc., Garden City, New York.

Rapoport, A.
1969   *House Form and Culture*. Prentice-Hall, Inc., Englewood Cliffs, New Jersey.

Ratzel, F.
1896   *The History of Mankind*. Macmillan and Company, London.

1899   *Anthropogeographie*. J. Engelhorn, Stuttgart.

Rosenbluth, A. and N. Wiener
1945   The Role of Models in Science. *Philosophy of Science*, Vol. 12, pp. 316-321.

Sage, A. P. and J. U. Melsa
1971   *System Identification.* Academic Press, New York.

Sauer, C.
1971   The Formative Years of Ratzel in the United States. *Annals of the Association of American Geographers*, Vol. 61, pp. 245-254.

Sayre, K. M. and F. J. Crosson
1963   *The Modeling of Mind.* Simon and Schuster, New York.

Semple, E. C.
1911   *Influences of Geographic Environment on the Basis of Ratzel's System of Anthropo-Geography.* Henry Holt, New York.

Shimek, B.
1911   The Prairies. *Bulletin of the Laboratory of Natural History, The State University of Iowa 6*, pp. 169-240. Iowa City.

Smith, C. S.
1953   Digging Up the Plains Indians' Past. *The University of Kansas Alumni Magazine*, Vol. 52, No. 4, pp. 4-5. Lawrence.

Smith, G. F.
1930   *Human History.* London.

Smith, P. E. L.
1972   Changes in Population Pressure in Archaeological Explanation. *World Archaeology*, Vol. 3, No. 3, pp. 5-18. London.

Sokal, R. R. and F. J. Rohlf
1969   *Biometry: The Principles and Practice of Statistics in Biological Research.* W. H. Freeman and Company, San Francisco.

Stanislawski, M. B.
1973   Review of *Archaeology as Anthropology: A Case Study*, by William A. Longacre (1970). *American Antiquity*, Vol. 38, No. 1, pp. 117-122.

Starbuck, W. H. and J. M. Dutton
1971   The History of Simulation Models. In, *Computer Simulation of Human Behavior*, edited by John Dutton and William Starbuck, pp. 9-102. John Wiley and Sons, Inc., New York.

Sterns, F. H.
1914   Ancient Lodge Sites on the Missouri in Nebraska. *American Anthropologist*, Vol. 16, pp. 135-137.

1915a   A Stratification of Cultures in Eastern Nebraska. *American Anthropologist*, Vol. 17, pp. 121-127.

1915b   The Archeology of Eastern Nebraska, With Special Reference to the Culture of the Rectangular Earth Lodges. MS, Ph.D. Dissertation, Harvard University, Cambridge.

Steward, J.
    1937   Ecological Aspects of Southwestern Society. *Anthropos*, Vol. 32, pp. 87-104.

    1938   Basin Plateau Aboriginal Socio-political Groups. *Bureau of American Ethnology, Bulletin 143*. Washington, D.C.

    1941   Culture Element Distribution: XIII. Nevada Shoshone. *University of California Anthropological Records*, Vol. 4, pp. 209-359.

Strong, W. D.
    1935   An Introduction to Nebraska Archeology. *Smithsonian Miscellaneous Collections*, Vol. 93, No. 10. Washington, D.C.

Taylor, W.
    1948   A Study of Archaeology. *American Anthropological Association Memoir 69*.

Thomas, D. H.
    1971   Prehistoric Subsistence-Settlement Patterns of the Reese River Valley, Central Nevada. MS, Ph.D. Dissertation, The University of California, Davis.

    1972   A Computer Simulation Model of Great Basin Subsistence and Settlement Patterns. In, *Models in Archaeology*, edited by David L. Clarke, pp. 671-704. Methuen and Company, Ltd., London.

    1973   An Empirical Test of Steward's Model for Great Basin Settlement Patterns. *American Antiquity*, Vol. 38, pp. 115-176.

    1974   An Archaeological Perspective on Shoshonean Bands. *American Anthropologist*, Vol. 76, No. 1, pp. 11-23.

Trewartha, G. T.
    1941   Climate and Settlement of the Subhumid Lands. In, Climate and Man, *1941 Yearbook of the United States Department of Agriculture*, edited by Gove Hambidge, pp. 167-176. Washington, D.C.

Trigger, B.
  1968   The Determinants of Settlement Patterns. In, *Settlement Archaeology*, edited by K. C. Chang, pp. 53-78. National Press Books, Palo Alto, California.

Tringham, R.
  1972   Introduction. In, *Man, Settlement, and Urbanism*, edited by Peter J. Ucko, Ruth Tringham, and G. W. Dimbleby, pp. *xix-xxviii*. Gerald Duckworth and Co., Ltd., London.

Turner, K.
  n.d.   Simulation of a Neo-Malthusian Model for Population Growth. (ms 1972).

Ucko, P. J., R. Tringham, and G. W. Dimbleby (Editors)
  1972   *Man, Settlement, and Urbanism.* Gerald Duckworth and Co., Ltd., London.

United States Department of Agriculture
  1941   Climates of the States: Iowa. In, Climate and Man, *1941 Yearbook of the United States Department of Agriculture,* edited by Gove Hambidge, pp. 862-872. Washington, D.C.

Vidal de la Blache, P.
  1926   *Principles of Human Geography.* New York.

Von Neumann, J. and O. Morgenstern
  1953   *Theory of Games and Economic Behavior.* Princeton University Press, Princeton.

Washburn, D. K.
  1972   An Analysis of the Spatial Aspects of the Site Locations of Pueblo I-III Sites Along the Middle Rio Puerco, New Mexico. MS, Ph.D. Dissertation, Columbia University, New York.

  1974   Nearest Neighbor Analysis of Pueblo I-III Settlement Patterns Along the Rio Puerco of the East, New Mexico. *American Antiquity*, Vol. 39, No. 2, pp. 315-335.

Weaver, J.
  1965   *Native Vegetation of Nebraska.* University of Nebraska Press, Lincoln.

  1968   *Prairie Plants and Their Environment: A Fifty Year Study.* University of Nebraska Press, Lincoln.

Wedel, W. R.
  1956   Changing Settlement Patterns in the Great Plains. In, Prehistoric Settlement Patterns in the New World, edited by G. R. Willey, *Viking Fund Publications in Anthropology 23*, pp. 81-92. New York.

  1959   An Introduction to Kansas Archeology. *Bureau of American Ethnology, Bulletin 174.* Washington, D.C.

  1961   *Prehistoric Man on the Great Plains.* University of Oklahoma Press, Norman.

Weiss, K. M.
  1973   Demographic Models for Anthropology. *Memoirs of the Society for American Archaeology*, No. 27.

Whallon, R.
  1972   The Computer in Archeology: A Critical Survey. *Computers and the Humanities,* Vol. 7, No. 1, pp. 29-45.

Will, G. F. and G. E. Hyde
  1917   *Corn Among the Indians of the Upper Missouri.* W. H. Miner, St. Louis.

Willey, G. R.
  1953   Prehistoric Settlement Patterns in the Viru Valley, Peru. *Bureau of American Ethnology, Bulletin 155.* Washington, D.C.

  1974   The Viru Valley Settlement Pattern Study. In, *Archaeological Researches in Retrospect*, edited by Gordon R. Willey, pp. 149-176. Winthrop Publishers, Inc., Cambridge.

Willey, G. R. (Editor)
  1956   Prehistoric Settlement Patterns in the New World. *Viking Fund Publications in Anthropology 23.* New York.

Willey, G. R. and P. Phillips
  1958   *Method and Theory in American Archaeology.* University of Chicago Press, Chicago.

Wilson, G. L.
  1917   Agriculture of the Hidatsa Indians: An Indian Interpretation. *University of Minnesota Studies in the Social Sciences*, No. 9. Minneapolis.

174

Wobst, H. M.
  1973   Editor's Foreword. In, Demographic Models for
          Anthropology, edited by H. Martin Wobst, *Memoirs of the
          Society for American Archaeology*, No. 27, pp. *vii-viii*.

  1974   Boundary Conditions for Paleolithic Social Systems: A
          Simulation Approach. *American Antiquity*, Vol. 39, No. 2, Pt. 1,
          pp. 147-178.

Wood, W. R.
  1969   Ethnographic Reconstructions. In, Two House Sites in the
          Central Plains: An Experiment in Archaeology, edited by W.
          Raymond Wood, *Plains Anthropologist Memoir 6*, Vol. 14, No.
          44, Pt. 2, pp. 102-108.

Wood, W. R. (Editor)
  1969   Two House Sites in the Central Plains: An Experiment in
          Archaeology. *Plains Anthropologist Memoir 6*, Vol. 14, No. 44, Pt.
          2.

Wyman, F. P.
  1970   *Simulation Modeling: A Guide to Using SIMSCRIPT*. John Wiley
          and Sons, Inc., New York.

Zawacki, A. A., and G. Hausfater
  1969   Early Vegetation of the Lower Illinois Valley. *Illinois State
          Museum Reports of Investigations*, No. 17. *Illinois Valley
          Archaeological Program Research Papers*, No. 1. Springfield.

Zimmerman, L. J.
  1971   The Glenwood Taxonomic Problem. MS, Master's Thesis, The
          University of Iowa, Iowa City.

Zimmerman, L. J. and D. Moore
  n.d.   Simulation of Settlement/Subsistence Systems: A Preliminary
          SIMSCRIPT Model for the Glenwood Locality. (ms 1973).

Zubrow, E. B. W.
  1971a   A Southwestern Test of an Anthropological Model of
          Population Dynamics. MS, Ph.D. Dissertation, The University
          of Arizona, Tucson.

  1971b   Carrying Capacity and Dynamic Equilibrium in the Prehistoric
          Southwest. *American Antiquity*, Vol. 36, No. 2, pp. 127-138.

Series Titles

Established in 1959, the Office of State Archaeologist has the primary responsibility for the discovery, excavation, and preservation of antiquities (Iowa Laws 305A). The State Archaeologist is appointed by the Board of Regents and serves on the faculty in Anthropology. Headquarters are at Eastlawn Building, The University of Iowa, Iowa City. Beginning in 1970, a series of reports and books has been issued on various investigations, describing and interpreting the discoveries. These studies are published in both hardbound and paperback editions and should be ordered from the University of Iowa Department of Publications, Iowa City 52242. The prices include postage.

The Davenport Conspiracy by Marshall McKusick. 1970, report 1, cloth (out of print), paperback $3.

The Kingston Oneota Site by Dean F. Straffin. 1971, report 2, cloth $5, paperback $2.

Prehistoric Investigations by Adrian Anderson, David Baerreis, Jerry Clark, Dale R. Henning, William M. Hurley, Marshall McKusick, Holmes A. Semken, Dean F. Straffin, and Larry J. Zimmerman. 1971, report 3, cloth $5, paperback $3. (Both out of print.)

The Grant Oneota Village by Marshall McKusick, Appendix by Holmes A. Semken. *Commentary* by David S. Brose, Alfred W. Bowers, David Baerreis, Hester A. Davis, Henry P. Field, Elizabeth J. Glenn, Dale R. Henning, William M. Hurley, Floyd G. Lounsbury, and G. Richard Peske. 1973, report 4, paperback $3.

Post-Conquest Developments in the Teotihuacan Valley, Mexico: Part 1, Excavations by Thomas H. Charlton. 1972, report 5, cloth $5, paperback $3.

Silver Creek Woodland Sites, Southwestern Wisconsin by William Hurley. 1975, report 6, paperback $4.

Physical Affiliations of the Oneota Peoples by Elizabeth J. Glenn. 1975, report 7, paperback $4.

The Iowa Northern Border Brigade by Marshall McKusick. 1975, report 8, cloth $5.50.

The Iowa Effigy Mound Manifestation: An Interpretive Model by R. Clark Mallam. 1976, report 9, paperback $4.

Prehistoric Locational Behavior: A Computer Simulation by Larry J. Zimmerman. 1977, report 10, paperback $4.